MW00957585

HABITS FOR SUCCESS

HOW TO CHANGE YOUR LIFE ONE STEP AT A TIME

DANIEL WALTER

HABITS FOR SUCCESS:
How to Change Your Life One Step at a Time
by Daniel Walter

© **Copyright 2022 by Daniel Walter**

All Rights Reserved.

No part of this publication may be reproduced, distributed, or transmitted in any form or by any means, including photocopying, recording, or other electronic or mechanical methods, without the prior written permission of the publisher, except in the case of brief quotations embodied in reviews and certain other noncommercial uses permitted by copyright law.

Disclaimer: This book is designed to provide accurate and authoritative information in regard to the subject matter covered. By its sale, neither the publisher nor the author is engaged in rendering psychological or other professional services. If expert assistance or counseling is needed, the services of a competent professional should be sought.

ISBN: 979-8352388778

ALSO BY DANIEL WALTER

The Power of Discipline:
How to Use Self-Control and Mental Toughness
to Achieve Your Goals

How to Stop Procrastinating: Powerful Strategies
to Overcome Laziness and Multiply Your Time

CONTENTS

INTRODUCTION

A re you tired of living in a never-ending cycle of under achievement? Have you got a bunch of goals written in a notebook that you keep revisiting year after year and promising to accomplish? Or maybe you've simply given up on the life of your dreams because you believe certain lifestyles are only for specific types of people. If you answered yes to any of these questions, I can definitely relate.

I spent ten years working as an investment banker, and at my peak I was earning $200,000 per year plus thousands of dollars in bonus payments. From the outside looking in, everything seemed great—I had the nice house, the nice car, and I went on expensive vacations twice a year with my friends. But I was broke! No one had any idea that, despite the fact that I was an investment banker, I was clueless about how to manage my *own* money. I was an impulsive spender; I went out to eat every evening, and I was out every weekend. Even though I paid them off every month, my credit cards were always maxed out, and I had no savings. My life was unraveling at the seams and I felt as if I had no control over it. Every month, I said the same thing: "I'm going to stop spending so much money and start saving." It never happened. I had this burning desire to keep buying the things I liked, and that was how I lived for many years.

I admired successful people like Bill Gates and Steve Jobs, and I often wondered if they had some special genes that made them successful. What did they have that I didn't? My curiosity led me to start investigating the lives of these people—and I was shocked to find that some of them had started out worse off than me. In fact, a lot of the most successful people in the world were raised in abject poverty. The more I read about them, the more I began to realize that success is about willpower, self-discipline, and good habits—all of which you can learn.

And that's exactly what I did. I studied the habits of the most successful people, and I implemented those habits. Today, I'm a bestselling author, I travel around the world speaking, and I actually have some money in the bank! However, it wasn't as simple as it sounds. What you will read about shortly is how difficult it is to break bad habits because they're so ingrained in us that they've actually become a part of our biology. But the good news is that if you're willing to put the work in, you can adopt the same habits as the successful people you admire, and build the same level of self-discipline as them, to ensure your dreams become a reality. In this book, you will learn:

- Why you've developed so many bad habits
- How to replace bad habits with good habits
- Why motivation isn't enough to achieve your dreams
- Why self-discipline is the only skill you need to become successful
- The importance of embracing failure
- How a consistent morning routine will change your life.

If you are tired of living below what you know you're capable of and are ready to start developing the habits that will catapult you to the next level, keep reading!

JOIN OUR PRODUCTIVITY GROUP

In order to maximize the value you receive from this book, I highly encourage you to join our tight-knit community on Facebook. Here, you will be able to connect and share productivity strategies that will enable you to continue your growth.

It would be great to connect with you there,

Daniel Walter

To Join, Visit:
www.pristinepublish.com/focusgroup

Or Scan the QR Code on Your Phone:

DOWNLOAD THE AUDIO VERSION OF THIS BOOK FOR FREE

If you love listening to audiobooks on the go or would enjoy a narration as you read along, I have great news for you. You can download the audiobook version of *Habits for Success* for FREE (Regularly $14.95) just by signing up for a FREE 30-day Audible Trial!

Visit: www.pristinepublish.com/audiobooks

Or Scan the QR Code on Your Phone:

YOUR FREE GIFT—
MASTER YOUR MORNING

Just thinking about the word "morning" can put a bad taste in people's mouths. A recent study found that one in four Americans hit the snooze button twice before getting out of bed. Forty-nine percent of the same sample stated that oversleeping is the main reason they are always late.

In other words, too many of us struggle with productivity—and there are very few people who jump out of bed as soon as their alarm goes off, excited about starting the day.

Take a couple of minutes and think about what your morning usually looks like…

So you don't feel alone in this, I'll start with what mine looked like a little less than three years ago:

- Set my alarm for 06:00 a.m., hit the snooze button until 07:00 a.m.
- Jump out of bed, shower, get dressed, and run out the door.
- Get a McDonald's breakfast and eat it on my way to work.
- Shout at the drivers on the road because it's their fault I woke up an hour late.
- Get to work with two minutes to spare.
- Sit at my desk stuffing my face with coffee and snacks all morning to keep my energy levels up.

But then I learned about the power of a consistent morning routine—and my life changed. I went from thinking I'd never achieve my dreams, to seeing them slowly manifest as I became confident that I could have anything I set my mind to. Let me start by explaining how healthy morning routines are created and why they make us more productive.

If I had to use an alternative word for "routine," I'd use the word "freedom" because that's what a routine gives us. Think about it like this: What's the first thing you do when you wake up in the morning? Most of you will say, "Brush my teeth." That's because it's a habit. Since childhood, we've been trained to brush our teeth as soon as we get out of bed in the morning, so we don't even think about it—we just do it. When you get in your car every morning to go to work, do you sit there thinking about how you're going to drive your vehicle? No—you just put your foot on the accelerator and go because it's a habit. But when you were first learning to drive, your driving instructor had to tell you what to do, and you had to think carefully about it when you were on the road. It may have taken a while, but you got there in the end, didn't you?

Establishing a morning routine works in the same way. Once it becomes a habit, and you're powering through your routine on autopilot, it will give you freedom because you will no longer struggle to succeed.

When we get down to basics, routines are the foundation of life; everything you do is routine, even if you don't think it is. Your bad morning habits of getting up late and having breakfast on the go have become a routine. The way you style your hair is a routine; the location you leave your shoes when you return home is a routine. Can you see my point? Everything is about routine.

The problem is that your current routines aren't doing you any favors. In fact, they're hindering you. Everything you do in the morning has become an enemy of progress, and the longer you continue living this way, the longer your success will be delayed. If you're anything like me, you probably don't know where to start when it comes to establishing a morning routine. I had no idea what I was doing when I started on this journey, but I had some good people in my life who gave me step-by-step instructions. And now I want to give them to you.

In my bonus e-book, *Master Your Morning*, you will learn about the seven habits you need to apply in order to become that person who jumps out of bed every morning raring to go. Here are three of them:

1. **A Bedtime Routine:** Sleep is one of the most important things you'll do every evening. Sleep is wonderful. We all love sleeping—which is the main reason so many of you hit the snooze button every morning! You've probably heard that healthy adults need eight hours of sleep a night, right? Arguably, this is true, but what you may not know is that the *quality* of your sleep is more important than the *quantity*. Do you wake up feeling drained and tired no matter how many hours of sleep you get? That's because you're not getting good-quality sleep. And the reason for that is you've got a terrible nighttime routine.

2. **Wake Up Early:** As you've just read, it's the quality of your sleep that will determine whether you wake up refreshed or not. The first step to dropping the terrible habit of smashing the snooze button every morning is establishing a good bedtime routine so you wake up

feeling refreshed and energized. Waking up early is an essential habit to cultivate if you want to succeed because it gives you a head start on the day.

3. **No Electronics:** Did you know that smartphone addiction is a real thing? I was addicted to my phone, and I had zero awareness of it. Every time it pinged, I would check to see who was messaging me, and I was always on social media. If you're going to get anywhere in life, kicking this habit is essential, and I'll show you how to do it.

Just by pondering these three habits, can you see where you're going wrong?

That's just a snippet of what's in store for you in *Master Your Morning*. You will have access to an abundance of helpful information that will kickstart your journey toward success and get you one step closer to living your dream life.

If you've got to that point where you're sick and tired of being sick and tired, this book is for you. It will equip you with everything you need in order to become more productive and start taking control of your life instead of letting life control you!

Get *Master Your Morning* for Free by Visiting

www.pristinepublish.com/morningbonus

Or Scan the QR Code on Your Phone:

CHAPTER 1:

HOW DO WE DEVELOP BAD HABITS?

Most of us were born and raised in well-meaning families who taught us to do the bare minimum. My parents encouraged me to get a good education and get into a career that offered attractive benefits and a decent retirement package. This is what their parents taught *them*, and so that was what they taught me. When they came home after a hard day's work, they spent the rest of the evening in front of the TV watching their favorite shows until bedtime. The last Friday of the month was our favorite day because we went to the local Chinese restaurant.

I'm not complaining; I had a decent life. But it was one devoid of purpose. I inherited my father's writing gift—my dad had a dream of becoming a famous author like Stephen King, and he spoke all the time about the book he was writing. Every year was the same: on New Year's Eve, he would declare that he was going to finish writing his book by December. For the first month, instead of watching TV after work, he'd go into his room, play classical music and type. We could hear the typewriter ricocheting through the house. But by February, he was back in the living room watching TV, his excuse being that he had writer's block. Well, that writer's block would last until the end of the year, and then he would declare the same thing. My father never became an author; he went to his grave with a half-completed book.

My grandparents discouraged my father from becoming an author. As far as they were concerned, it wouldn't bring in a stable income and it would be impossible for him to raise a family with any pride. They believed success was only for the privileged, and not for "simple" people like them. My dad chose to honor his parents' wishes and become an accountant, subsequently spending his entire life complaining about his job.

When I expressed an interest in writing, my father did exactly what his parents had done to him and encouraged me not to follow my dreams. I too honored my father's wishes for many years—until I realized that I had become him. As much as I loved him, I didn't want to die without reaching my full potential and blessing the world with the gift I knew I'd been born with. I am grateful that my father lived to see me achieve the dream that he didn't.

When I first attempted to start writing, I was literally following in my dad's footsteps; I would make a New Year's resolution, bury myself in it, then give up by February. I too started to believe that success was only for the privileged—but that was only because I didn't understand that I had been programmed mediocrity. But things changed for me once I learned why my bad habits were keeping me stuck, and how I could break free from them. As you read in the introduction, I had a plethora of issues, so it's literally a miracle that I am where I am today.

THE SUBCONSCIOUS AND THE CONSCIOUS MIND

The brain is the most complicated and powerful organ in the body. It is made up of two parts: the conscious and the subconscious mind. You can compare the subconscious mind to the hard drive on a computer. It permanently stores every memory we have in life, and its capacity is unlimited. According to experts, by the age of 21, the subconscious mind has stored over one hundred times the contents of the *Encyclopedia Britannica*. When an old person is hypnotized, they can clearly remember everything that took place in their life 50 years prior. The unconscious memory is perfect; the conscious memory isn't—which is why we are prone to forgetting things.

The subconscious mind retrieves and stores information; its job is to make sure you respond in the way you've been programmed. Everything you say and do should line up with what's been stored in the subconscious mind. The subconscious mind is subjective; it doesn't analyze and evaluate the information it receives, but simply obeys the commands sent by the conscious mind. The conscious mind acts as a gardener, and the subconscious mind is the garden. The gardener plants seeds in the garden, and those seeds take root and start growing. So, if you are not sowing good seeds, don't expect to reap a good harvest.

A homeostatic impulse built into the subconscious mind regulates your body temperature so that it's set at 98.6 degrees F. It also keeps your heart beating, and it keeps you breathing. Your automatic nervous system, as well as the many chemicals and cells in your body, work in perfect harmony so you function the way you're supposed to. The homeostatic impulse also keeps you thinking and acting in a way that's consistent with the things you've said or done in the past. Your subconscious mind has stored your comfort zones, and it works hard to keep you there. That's why you find it so hard to maintain a new habit. Every year for about five years straight, I said the same things: I was going to write my book; I was going to stop spending so much money; I was going to lose weight. I'd start writing, stop spending, and sign up to the gym. I'd be consistent for a month and then slip back into my old habits. Why? Because my subconscious mind kept pulling me back into my comfort zone. When you start something new and get that feeling of discomfort and fear, it's a sign that your subconscious mind has been activated. The bottom line is that if your life is led by your bad habits, making a conscious, determined effort to change them isn't going to help. You've got to challenge them at the level of the subconscious mind, or you'll keep falling back into old patterns. The good news is that no matter how long your bad habits have been controlling your life, you can reprogram your subconscious mind for success. You'll learn how to do this in Chapter 10.

WHY CHANGE IS SO DIFFICULT

Research suggests that approximately 70 percent of smokers would like to quit because they know it's killing them. Today, it's against the law for tobacco companies to sell their products without putting warnings on their packaging about the dangers of smoking. Some of the images used are very explicit, showing the damage smoke causes to the organs in the body. But despite the graphic images and the lung cancer statistics, people are still smoking. Alcohol and drug abusers have a powerful love affair with their addictions, even though it's killing them and tearing families, friends, and loved ones apart.

Obesity is an epidemic in America, but people keep consuming an unhealthy diet even though it could kill them. It's easy to become judgmental when you don't have an obvious addiction. You'll hear the comments when an overweight person supersizes their meal, or when a drug addict is seen begging for money in the streets. But why have I never heard any nasty comments about my spending habits? When I was at the till ringing up thousands of dollars on my credit cards, I didn't hear anyone sniggering that I need to stop spending so much money. When I was sat in front of the TV for hours on end when I was supposed to be working on my course, I didn't hear anyone sniggering that I needed to stop watching so much television.

Why? Because overspending and indulging in mind-numbing activities are not considered addictions. But science proves that they are (I'll talk about that shortly). The inability to fulfil your highest potential isn't frowned upon because the majority of people don't. But the funny thing is that we all talk about it. My friends and I would always sit and discuss what we wanted to achieve, but none of us ever made the effort to chase after our dreams. Or we would start, and a few months later we had an excuse about why we had to stop. Why is it that humans find it so difficult to follow through? Let's take a look.

Scientists have spent years studying what happens to the brain when habits form. They've found a lot of interesting information about the process that takes place in the brain, and there are proven scientific explanations as to why it's so difficult to break bad habits once they're formed. We develop habits through repetition. You don't need to think about brushing your teeth in the morning, because your parents taught you how to do that when you were a child. I doubt there are many people in the world who struggle to brush their teeth. When you were learning how to drive, you found it difficult, but the more you practiced, the easier it became, and now you can get in the car and drive without thinking about it. Behavioral psychologist Nora Volkow states that certain behaviors are easy once they become automatic because the brain doesn't think consciously about the activity—it just does it.

Habits also develop when there is a corresponding positive feeling associated with the activity. For example, it feels good when you eat unhealthy foods, smoke, gamble, take drugs, drink alcohol, or check social media. According to neurobiologist Dr. Russell Poldrack, good and bad habits are built on the same type of mechanism, but there is one major difference—which is what makes pleasure-based habits so difficult to break. Pleasurable behaviors trigger the brain to release the feel-good hormone dopamine. When you keep repeating the behavior and experiencing the pleasurable effects of dopamine, the habit is strengthened. I had a spending habit, and when I wasn't spending money, I experienced a craving to do so. That's because dopamine creates cravings—when the body feels good, it wants to continue feeling good.

What I noticed was that I would get the craving to spend, yet once I had made my purchase, I no longer felt good. So, it was the *thought of spending* that made me feel good, not the actual act. Once the money had gone from my account, I was left with a sinking feeling of regret. The same happens when you're addicted to fast food: the body craves it; the thought of it is so exciting that you go out and buy it; whilst you're eating it you feel great because it tastes delicious—but once it's finished, you feel awful because unhealthy food isn't designed to make you feel good. Once you're addicted to something, your brain starts working against you when you try and overcome bad habits because it's become hardwired to crave the thing you are trying to resist.

WE ARE HARDWIRED TO TAKE THE PATH OF LEAST RESISTANCE

One of the most insightful books I've ever read is called *The Path of Least Resistance* by Robert Fritz. He provides some astounding truths as to why humans prefer taking the easy way out. Bad habits are comforting. We like the feeling of lying in a warm, cozy bed instead of getting up at the crack of dawn to work out. We like the feeling of being entertained when we are scrolling through social media. Fritz compares humans to rivers because we travel through life taking the path of least resistance. As you've probably experienced, there will come a time when you want to change the direction of your flow. You want to start working out, develop better relationships, change your eating habits, or become more productive. You get into a routine, and you do well for a while, but after a few weeks, you return to your old habits and you just can't seem to stay on track. Why? According to Fritz, it's the law of nature: humans have been hardwired to take the path of least resistance.

Fritz also believes that we all have an underlying structure to our lives, and this determines the path we take. In the same way a riverbed determines the path that the water flows through it, your life structures determine your path of least resistance. You may or may not be aware of your life structures, but they are there. Whether there is water flowing or not, the structure of the river remains the same.

WHY MOTIVATION IS NOT ENOUGH

When I was a child, my sisters and I woke up every Sunday morning to watch *Karate Kid*. We loved it; it was so inspiring, and we wanted to become karate champions. After the movie, we would practice all the moves and make a pact that we'd do press-ups and sit-ups every morning so we'd be fit enough to compete in a tournament one day. By Wednesday, we all had an excuse as to why we couldn't wake up an hour earlier for our practice. We eventually grew out of wanting to become karate champions, but we didn't grow out of not following through on our commitments. We were children, and we would laugh about our lack of dedication; we genuinely thought it was funny. It wasn't until years later that I learned why we couldn't keep ourselves motivated to become karate champions.

It was because motivation doesn't last. When we are motivated, we are driven to take action. Basically, motivation is a feeling—it's the adrenaline rush you get when you hear a powerful speech or watch an inspiring movie. And as I'm sure you're aware, feelings change. Another reason motivation doesn't last is because when we face challenges, it weakens. Humans are led by their emotions, and while our forebrains are highly sophisticated, it's our limbic brain that dictates our actions. Everything we do is driven by our unconscious desires. The limbic brain is responsible for our physical survival and the overall regulation of our body. Its main function is to preserve our basic survival needs such as reproduction, breathing, and movement. Additionally, it controls unconscious actions and doesn't like change.

When we are trying to develop a habit, our efforts are hijacked by the reptilian brain because it's been programmed to act in one way. As I've mentioned, we do things on autopilot, and we are directed by our instincts. If you've been programmed to enjoy comfort rather than discipline, you are always going to go in that direction and give in to gratification instead of thinking logically about the urges you are having. According to motivational speaker Jim Rohn, motivation gets you started, but habit is the driving force behind getting you to your destination.

To develop good habits, you need self-discipline. I will discuss the importance of self-discipline in Chapter 2.

CHAPTER 2:

WHY SELF-DISCIPLINE IS THE MOST IMPORTANT HABIT TO MASTER

Did you know that there are people in the world more talented than the best singers, dancers, and actors? There are people in the world who are smarter than Bill Gates and Warren Buffett. But one thing these people *don't* have is discipline. You see, you can be naturally gifted, but if you don't have the discipline to refine those gifts and become an expert, you'll never prosper. Kobe Bryant (may he rest in peace) was and still is considered one of the greatest athletes of our generation. Not just because he was a naturally gifted basketball player, but because of his relentless work ethic and unstoppable mindset. In 2016, he accepted the Icon Award at the ESPYs and gave a powerful speech in front of his fellow athletes. One of the things he said was that he didn't get to where he was because of his talent, but because he woke up at 4:00 a.m. every morning. He had a dream and he was persistent in ensuring that it became his reality—but he had to make many sacrifices for it, and one of those sacrifices involved waking up at 4:00 a.m. to practice.

Kobe Bryant was known as one of the greatest athletes of all time because of his dedication to his dream. When we look at successful people, we're looking at a finished product. What we don't see are the years of blood, sweat, and tears it took to build a foundation strong enough to hold the weight of such a powerful vision. We see the glitter, the gold, and the glamor. The mansions, cars, designer clothes, gold medals, and sold-out concerts. But what we don't see is the work that goes into it—and that's what most people are not prepared to do. In order to become successful, you've got to develop some very uncomfortable habits, you've got to outwork everyone else, and you've got to outwork yourself.

In his book *Change Your Habits, Change Your Life*, author Tom Corley studied the daily habits of 233 millionaires. But he didn't stop there; he also studied the habits of 128 people who earn less than $35,000 per year. And what he found was that your habits will determine whether or not you succeed in life. Let's take a look at the good habits of highly successful people, and the bad habits that are keeping you at the bottom of the totem pole.

Wealthy People Are Early Risers: Approximately 50 percent of the millionaires in Corley's study woke up at least three hours before their workday began. Most of them spent that time exercising, planning the day ahead, or tackling personal projects. Corley states that waking up at 05:00 a.m. to get the most important things on your to-do list out of the way gives you control over your life. It provides you with a sense of confidence that you are in fact the captain of your ship.

Wealthy People Read Books: Eighty-eight percent of the respondents in Corley's research said that they spent at least 30 minutes a day on self-improvement by reading. Wealthy people do not read for entertainment purposes, but to educate themselves. They prefer reading books on personal development, biographies, and history. Self-made billionaire Warren Buffett says he spends approximately six hours per day reading, and that it has been the most important habit he's developed.

Wealthy People Exercise: Studies have found that exercise gives you mental clarity and improves your motivation. Corley reports that 76 percent of the respondents in his research spent at least 30 minutes a day engaging in aerobic exercise such as walking, biking, or jogging. Many successful business leaders make time to work out every day. For example, Richard Branson wakes up at 05:00 am, goes cycling, or plays tennis. He states that adding exercise to his routine has maximized his productivity.

Wealthy People Are Thinkers: Wealthy people spend 15 to 30 minutes per day thinking. Corley discovered that they think in isolation as a part of their morning routine. This time is spent processing everything that's going on in their lives and strategizing for future events. They reflect on their personal relationships, their health, and their careers. According to research, having quiet time to evaluate your thoughts is linked to stress reduction.

Wealthy People Pursue Their Goals: Success is not an accident; wealthy people make a plan to get rich and then take the action required to make it happen. Corley found that 80 percent of the wealthy people in his study were obsessed with pursuing and achieving their goals. They evaluated their long- and short-term goals daily. Unbeknownst to many of us, the majority of people spend their lives fulfilling other people's dreams. Climbing up the corporate ladder only benefits the owner of that company. Wealthy people put a ladder up against their own wall and climb to the top of their own castle.

Wealthy People Spend Time Being Inspired: Successful people make a point of limiting their exposure to toxic, negative individuals who drain their energy and stunt their motivation. Corley found that the wealthy people in his study connected with people who inspired them to achieve their goals and to remain on the path of continuous improvement.

Wealthy People Have More Than One Stream of Income: Wealthy people generally have more than one source of income. Corley found that, prior to making their first million dollars, respondents had at least three streams of income such as real estate or other investments. It's important to have multiple sources of income because the economy is not always going to be stable. You can lose a job the moment your company goes bust. If you own your own company, you can lose that income if there is no longer a demand for your products or services. Therefore, the most effective way to stay ahead of the game is to have multiple sources of income.

Wealthy People Get Enough Sleep: Sleep is important because it rejuvenates the body. Albert Einstein said that he got at least ten hours of sleep a night. The assumption is that rich people don't sleep; instead they spend every last hour of their day on money-making endeavors. Corley found the opposite to be true—a whopping 89 percent of the wealthy people in his study got seven or more hours of sleep a night. Research suggests that sleep is essential to success because it affects creative thinking and memory function.

Wealthy People Value Their Time: The most important asset in the world is time. You can re-earn lost money, you can get your health back if you fall ill, you can buy another house if it gets repossessed. But time is one thing you can never buy back—which is why wealthy people value it so much. Corley found that wealthy people don't waste their time scrolling through social media, or binge-watching programs on Netflix. They also avoid people who waste their time. I am very intentional about who I choose to spend my time with, even family members. The way I see it, if people are not adding to your life, they're taking from it, and if you want to achieve your goals, you can't afford to associate with people who feel they've got the right to monopolize your time with foolishness.

Now, let's take a look at the habits of the men and women in Corley's study who earned less than $35,000 per year. He referred to them as *poverty habits*. Here are some of them:

Remaining in Your Comfort Zone: Growth doesn't happen in comfort. Becoming successful is the most uncomfortable thing you'll ever do. If you want to achieve your goals, you'll need to get comfortable with being uncomfortable. Corley found that poor people like to blend in; they want to be accepted, and they don't like standing out from the crowd. But the inability to separate yourself from the masses is one of the main reasons people don't achieve anything. The average person enjoys being in familiar surroundings, and they don't like leaving their comfort zone. In contrast, wealthy people enjoy uncertainty—that's where they find comfort because that's the place of unlimited potential. To become wealthy, you've got to take risks, and most people are not willing to do that.

Job Dissatisfaction: Poor people generally hate their jobs, but because of the perceived security a job provides, they remain in employment they feel dissatisfied with. Leaving your house every morning to go to a job you can't stand will cause you to become frustrated, stressed, and unsatisfied with life. Ultimately, it will affect your chances of becoming wealthy because you won't have the energy to do anything other than work in a job that makes you miserable and complain about it. Successful people chase their passions, and that's where they get the most satisfaction. Passion is more important than skills, intelligence, and education because that's what drives you. Getting out of bed in the morning becomes exciting when you look forward to the work you are doing.

Spending Too Much: Poor people don't have any financial discipline; they acquire liabilities instead of assets. Ninety-five percent of the people in Corley's study had no savings, and they had massive debts because they refused to live within their means. As a result, they had no money to send their children to college, for retirement, or to pursue the opportunities that could improve their financial situation. Spending more money than you earn creates an endless cycle of poverty.

Avoiding Feedback: Poor people don't like constructive criticism because it requires self-evaluation. It goes back to staying in your comfort zone; when a manager, mentor or friend gives you feedback, it means you've got to take action and make the necessary improvements to get on track. Making improvements in any area of your life means stepping outside your comfort zone, and the average person wants to remain comfortable.

Procrastination: There is no denying that everyone procrastinates on tasks they don't enjoy. But poor people spend way too much time procrastinating. Corley states that procrastination prevents some of the most talented people from becoming successful. Additionally, according to bestselling author Napoleon Hill, wealthy people make decisions quickly; they follow their instincts—if it feels right, they run with it, and if not, they look for another option. Procrastination is one of the main reasons that people struggle financially. It ruins your credibility with employers and work colleagues when you rush to get work done at the last minute, and it affects the quality of your output.

Negative Thinking: Again, negative thinking is something that we all experience no matter how wealthy we might be. The difference between the rich and the poor is that the rich don't let it define them, and they don't allow it to stop them from getting things done. They quickly reframe their thoughts and keep things moving. On the other hand, poor people are driven by their negative thinking. They won't apply for promotions, start a business, or look for a higher-paying job, because they have convinced themselves they are incapable.

Watching Too Much Television: Seventy-seven percent of the poor people in Corley's study spent over one hour each day watching TV. On the other hand, sixty-six percent of the millionaires in his study spent less than one hour a day watching television. He concluded that the poor prefer to be entertained than educated, whereas the rich prefer to be educated instead of entertained. One of the hallmarks of self-made millionaires is the productive use of their time.

Associating With Negative People: Eighty-six percent of the wealthy people who took part in Corley's research made a habit of associating with people who were just as driven and motivated as them. When you associate with people who are constantly striving to achieve their goals and become the best versions of themselves, you have no time to be toxic and negative. However, only four percent of the poor people in Corley's study associated with people who directed their energy towards success and positivity. Ninety-six percent associated with negative, toxic individuals.

Drinking Too Much Alcohol: There is nothing wrong with drinking alcohol—the occasional beer or glass of wine isn't going to hurt. But fifty-four percent of the poor people in Corley's study drank more than two glasses of alcohol per day. Eighty-four percent of the millionaires drank less than two glasses of alcohol per day. Research has found that too much alcohol has a negative effect on your memory, and it clouds your judgment.

Unhealthy Eating: Ninety percent of the poor people in Corley's study ate more than three hundred calories from junk food every day. Sixty-nine percent ate takeaway more than three times per week. Sixty-nine percent ate candy more than three times a week, and 66 percent of the participants were at least 30 pounds overweight. Wealthy people invest in their health by eating the right foods and doing regular exercise. A healthy diet not only helps you keep the weight off, it gives you more energy and boosts your brainpower.

Gambling: People gamble and play the lottery because they want to make quick money. But getting rich quick is rare, and the people who do tend to lose the money just as quickly as they made it. Financial success requires relentless effort, initiative, and time. People who gamble have convinced themselves that it's a shortcut to wealth. In Corley's study, he found that 77 percent of poor people played the lottery every week, and fifty-two percent gambled on sports at least once a week. In comparison, 94 percent of rich people didn't play the lottery, and 84 percent didn't gamble on sports. Instead of relying on get-rich-quick schemes, wealthy people rely on developing the habit of chasing their dreams.

It's also important to mention that having the discipline to achieve your goals isn't enough. You've also got to have the discipline to *maintain* your goals. There are plenty of people who achieved a measure of success and lost it because they became complacent and undisciplined once they got to the top. Today, my life might look easier than it did ten years ago, but I now work harder to maintain what I've got. That's why the habits mentioned above must become a lifestyle and not just a stepping stone to success.

How to Develop Self-discipline

You've just read about the difference between the habits of the rich and the poor. The main difference between these two groups is self-discipline. In reality, everyone is disciplined to a degree, but some people are just disciplined in the wrong things. The poor person has developed a habit of sitting in front of the TV every night, while the rich person has developed a habit of reading a book or exercising. The question is, how do you become disciplined in the right things? First, let's define self-discipline.

What is Self-Discipline? In short, it's the ability to do what you know you need to do when you don't feel like doing it. Self-discipline is about drive, determination, resolve, willpower, self-regulation, and self-control. As far as I'm concerned, it's the superpower that trumps all superpowers because without self-discipline, all other superpowers are ineffective. All experts stress the importance of self-discipline. It's the most important ingredient in anything you want to do, whether you want to improve your relationships, manage your emotions better, be more positive, get promoted, procrastinate less, be more productive, spend less, exercise more, eat better, or lose weight. There are several benefits to self-discipline. Here are some of them:

It Helps You Control Your Emotions: When you get angry, upset, or frustrated, your first instinct is to react to how you're feeling—but that's not a good idea. Anger is a powerful emotion, and even the most unlikely people have killed because of it. I know that I've said some pretty terrible things when I've been angry. Unfortunately, once those words are released, you can't take them back. When you're self-disciplined, you can control your emotions better. That doesn't mean you're not going to feel angry, upset, or frustrated, but it does mean you'll be more likely to process your emotions before reacting to them. In this way, you are able to respond more appropriately to the situation.

Improved Financial Health: Despite the fact that I was earning $200,000 per year, I was always broke. Why? Because I had no self-discipline; I spent money like I had a never-ending stream of it running through my bank account. Meals out cost $300, I booked weekends away and blew $5K in two days! I bought the most expensive suits, my spending was out of control, and I found it very difficult to get my finances in order. We all know that spending money feels good—buying those new, shiny items is always pleasurable. But living within your means, saving for a rainy day, and planning for the future will be of more benefit to you in the long run. I didn't like the idea of financial discipline; I assumed it meant I had to live like a pauper and put total restrictions on my life. But it wasn't as bad as I thought—I just had to get into the habit of sticking to a budget and saving a percentage of my salary every month. It sounds simple, but when you're used to blowing thousands in one go, you are going to struggle. Although I did get some satisfaction out of the fact that I knew I could afford what I really wanted but I was choosing not to indulge. It was also really satisfying to see money piling up in my bank account.

You Will Have Fewer Regrets: This is connected to controlling your emotions. When you don't have any self-discipline, you make bad choices; you don't think before you speak, which means you are more likely to blurt out something embarrassing at the wrong time. Instead, you will spend time gathering all the necessary information before making a decision, which means you won't make choices based on your opinion or emotion, but on facts.

Success in Your Field: Whether you're a student or an investment banker like I was, success in any area requires hard work. When you are not self-disciplined, you'll never reach your highest potential—it's impossible. Becoming the best version of yourself requires extreme discipline. I always did the bare minimum and got away with it because I was naturally intelligent. But I could have gone a lot further in my field if I had put the work in. At the time, I didn't think I needed to, and I wasn't willing to do it. But that's not how people get recognized in their field. I was one of those people who would turn my nose up at employees who got promoted ahead of me. I could never understand it—I assumed my qualifications were enough. But the people who got promoted were the ones who were always on time for work, stayed after hours, and took the necessary courses to improve their skills. That type of work ethic requires discipline, and it will get you noticed.

Improved Relationships: I was the most unreliable person in my family. If I said I'd be there at 6:00 p.m., I'd arrive at 8:00 p.m. If I said I'd call at 12:00 noon, I'd call at 2:00 p.m. I just couldn't stick to anything, and it really rubbed people up the wrong way. I knew I was unreliable, and I didn't think about it until I started doing it to my mentor and he pulled me up on it. Mike had me put myself in the shoes of the people I was always letting down. When I thought about it like that, I realized how badly I'd disappointed people. It was a running joke that I was untrustworthy—we all laughed about it—but even though my family had just learned to accept it, deep down, it bothered them. I found this out when we had a heart-to-heart after I decided to get my life on track. To begin with, they didn't believe I was going to change—and they had every right not to. It was up to me to prove myself because I'd let them down so many times. There were definitely a few bumps along the road, but I got there in the end, and today they know my word is my bond.

The assumption is that self-discipline is an innate characteristic that some people have and others don't. That's not the case—it's learned behavior. The problem is that the majority of people are not raised in homes where there is an emphasis on self-discipline. I know this to be true from my own personal experience. My parents spoke about it all the time, but they didn't model it because they didn't know how. I was basically trained to do the bare minimum. I didn't tap into my highest potential until I was in my late thirties. My mentor taught me about the importance of self-discipline and how to develop it, so here are some tips:

Motivate Yourself: Have you ever noticed that when you're excited about something, you don't struggle to achieve it—you just get on with it because you're passionate, energetic, and enthusiastic about it? Let's say you've got a vacation coming up and you know you want to look good in your bikini or swimming trunks, and so you set yourself a weight-loss goal. You fly out of bed at 5:00 a.m. when that alarm goes off. You guzzle down gallons of water as if it were your favorite soda, and you feast on that salad as if it were a Big Mac. Motivation is the reason we do things. *The power of why* is a concept that is spoken about by leadership expert Simon Sinek. When you have a clear understanding of why you want to achieve something, you are more likely to stay focused and achieve it.

Before you start on your journey of building better habits, tap into your *why*. I wanted to develop better habits because I wanted more out of life for myself and my future family. I also had a deep desire to help other people, but I didn't feel that I was in a position to do so because I was still struggling myself. Once I had identified my why, putting what I was learning into practice became a lot easier.

Develop a Morning Routine: In his book *The Miracle Morning*, Hal Elrod says that the way you start your day has a major impact on your success in life. A focused and productive morning leads to a focused and productive day. The more productive you are, the more you get done. But most people don't have focused and productive mornings; they hit the snooze button over and over again so that they have just enough time to take a shower and get dressed. Then they stop off at McDonald's or Starbucks for breakfast so they've got just enough energy to make it until lunch. They grab a pizza for lunch, and then rush home after work to eat another unhealthy meal while they sit in front of the TV. How can you expect to achieve your goals when you live like this? Hal Elrod wrote his book because that was how *he* lived his life until he developed the habit of a morning routine. He went from being terribly depressed, broke, and unhealthy, to being an international keynote speaker, a successful businessman, an ultra-marathon runner, and a bestselling author. He has now transformed the lives of thousands of others by teaching them about the importance of developing the habit of a morning routine.

There are six variables in Hal's morning equation: Silence, Affirmations, Visualization, Exercise, Reading, and Scribing. Together, they form the acronym: SAVERS. He put them together after evaluating the lives of the most successful and productive people in the world. Of course, you can make changes to the equation, but use Hal's method as a template. Try out different things and see what works best for you.

I can say with confidence that one of the most important keys to success is your morning routine. I have personally developed the following morning habits:

- Meditation for ten minutes
- A 30-minute run
- A cold shower
- Reading for 15 minutes

And I do this EVERY morning! I must admit that it took me several months to develop the habit, but I got there in the end. My aim was to get to 90 days straight because, according to research, once you repeat something for 90 days in a row, it becomes a lifestyle. I broke the 90 days into ten days at a time. If I fell off (which I did often), I'd have to go back to day one. I'll never forget when I made it to 90 days—something clicked in me; I just knew my life was about to change. And it most certainly did, from that day forwards.

Get Rid of Temptations: My guilty pleasure was my TV. After a long, hard day at work, I felt that I deserved to sit in front of the soapbox for a few hours. The problem was that I did this every night, and on the weekends. Every time I said I was going to work on my book, or my online financial management course, I'd watch TV instead. This went on for weeks. I kept promising myself I would only watch one show, but that one show turned into two, then three, then it was time to go to bed, and I would promise myself I would get it done the next day. But the next day never came. In the end, I took the television off the wall and gave it to my brother. I motivated myself by agreeing to get another TV when I'd achieved a certain level of success.

A study conducted by Cornell University found that our choices are affected by our environment. They discovered that women who kept a box of cereal on the counter were an average of 20 pounds heavier than those who didn't. Also, women who kept soft drinks on their counter were an average of 24 to 26 pounds heavier than the women who didn't. Finally, women who kept fruit on their counter were an average of 13 pounds lighter than the women who didn't. In other words, if your goal is to lose weight, don't have junk food anywhere near you. If you've got a deadline to meet and you find it difficult to work from home, go to the library, or stay at work for an extra couple of hours. Don't waste your time trying to fight the temptations in your environment—just remove them, or remove yourself.

Set Yourself a Deadline, Challenge, or Goal: When one year had passed and I hadn't written my book or finished the financial management course that should have taken me three months to complete, I decided that enough was enough—I was going to finish it within a month, and that was the end of the discussion. It was May 2nd. I called my mentor and told him that if I hadn't graduated from the class by June 2nd, I would owe him $1000. It was tight, but I could do it if I put my mind to it—and besides, I really didn't want to pay out $1000. I went to the 24-hour library every day for 26 days in a row, and I did it: I finished the course before the deadline I'd set for myself. If you want to get something done, set a deadline, challenge, or goal and get on with it.

Do the Most Difficult Things First: In his book *The 7 Habits of Highly Effective People*, Stephen Covey talks about getting the most difficult and important tasks out of the way first. The reason being is that we only have a certain amount of willpower, and as the day goes on, we become less focused. Have you ever noticed how productive you are during the first three or four hours at work, and by 2:00 p.m. you're yawning, going for toilet breaks every 20 minutes, and checking your watch constantly? When you get the most difficult things done first, you increase your chances of completing your to-do list because it doesn't take much willpower to do the small things. The problem with small tasks is that even though they don't take a lot of willpower, they can take a lot of time, which means when you do them first, you are less productive on the difficult task, and it will take you a lot longer to complete.

Embrace Failure: "What the hell does embracing failure have to do with self-discipline?" I hear you asking. The answer is *everything!* Fear is paralyzing, and it will stop you from moving before you've even taken the first step. One of the acronyms for fear is: False Evidence Appearing Real. In other words, you've made up a scenario in your head and spent so much time thinking about it, you've convinced yourself it's real. According to the National Institute of Mental Health, 75 percent of people rank public speaking as their number one fear. In other words, people fear speaking in front of an audience more than they fear death! That's insane…

I once fell into this percentage. But the kicker was that I'd never spoken in front of anyone before—so how did I know I wouldn't be good at it? Because the idea of speaking in front of a group of people didn't sit well with me, I made up all types of scenarios in my head. What if I forgot what I was going to say? What if I had sweat patches? What if the audience thought I was an idiot? And so on, and so on. When I finally plucked up the courage to speak in public, I realized my fears were unfounded. I was nervous, but I did a good job. In fact, I got a standing ovation. So, why should we embrace failure? Because your fear of it is not based on experience; you learn more from failure than you do from success. There are some life principles you'll learn in the gutter that you'll never have access to on the mountaintop. Failure teaches you what not to do; as long as you don't give up when you fail, failure will always act as a guiding light.

Still not convinced that you should embrace failure? Let me tell you a story about my favorite motivational speaker, Les Brown.

One of his life goals was to buy his adoptive mother a house. When he finally made enough for a deposit, he went looking for the perfect home, and he found it. He was so excited to move her from her roach-infested apartment into a mansion. But no sooner had he signed the papers and handed over the money than he received a foreclosure notice because the previous owner had taken out a loan on the house and not paid it back. He had to pay $30,000 within 30 days or the bank would take the house. He wasn't able to raise that money, and he was forced to move his mother back into the roach-infested apartment he had just moved her out of. This was Brown's first house, and in his haste to move in, he had failed to do a title check. If he had, he would have found out that there was a debt on the house. The good news is that 90 days later, Brown made enough money to move his mother into a bigger and better home. Why? Because he embraced failure. He accepted that he'd made a mistake, he learned from it, brushed himself off and focused on his goal of buying his mother a house, and that's what he did.

There are plenty more examples of people who have failed and gone on to have massive success. But the moral of the story is that failure is only the end if you decide that it's going to be.

Self-discipline covers many areas, and one of them is thinking. According to James Geary, we are what we think, and if you want to develop good habits, your thought process needs to be in alignment with what you want. You will learn more about this in Chapter 3.

CHAPTER 3:

CHANGE YOUR THINKING— CHANGE YOUR LIFE

My friends and I used to mock the advocates of positive thinking. I found people like Tony Robbins and Deepak Chopra highly irritating. To me, being positive when your life was crumbling to pieces made no sense whatsoever. I thought it was highly unrealistic to walk around with a smile on your face when you didn't know how you were going to make it through the rest of the month. But once I got my head out of the clouds, I learned that positive thinking wasn't about living in denial about the reality of your situation, but about reframing it so you can handle it better. Before I get into how you can change your thinking, let's take a look at some of the benefits of positive thinking.

Improved Physical Health: It isn't known whether positive thinkers are more likely to take better care of their health through regular exercise and a healthy diet, but research suggests that optimists are healthier. There may be several reasons for this, including the fact that they don't experience as much stress, and because of the way they think, when they do experience it, they are better able to cope. Whatever the reason, optimists appear to be healthier than pessimists. Studies have found that they are:

- Unlikely to die from cardiovascular disease
- Less likely to catch colds/flu because their immune systems are stronger
- Likely to recover faster from illnesses or injuries
- Likely to live longer.

One study monitored 70,000 women between 2004 to 2012 and found that those with a positive attitude towards life were at less risk of dying from conditions such as:

- Respiratory disease
- Infection
- Cancer
- Stroke
- Heart disease.

Improved Mental Health: People with a positive mindset are less likely to suffer from mental health problems such as anxiety and depression. Overall, they experience better psychological health in comparison to pessimists. Although positive thinking isn't a cure for mental health problems, when you look at life through a positive lens, you are better equipped to handle difficult life events.

Better Coping Mechanisms for Stress: Stress is a part of life; it's something we can't avoid. People lose their jobs, have conflicts at home, work, or with friends, a death in the family etc. Whatever the situation, what matters is how you handle it. Studies have found that optimists are more likely to deal with negative circumstances by strategizing and finding ways to rectify the situation. They don't waste their time complaining about the things they can't change, why the situation occurred, or whose fault it was. Pessimists take the opposite approach and lament instead of trying to fix it.

A More Active Social Life: Think about it like this: who do you prefer to be around—positive or negative people? Even negative people like being around good vibes because it makes them feel better. Optimists laugh a lot, they can always see the light at the end of the tunnel, and they've just got a good attitude in general. People like this generally have more friends and get invited to more social engagements.

More Successful: When you expect good things to happen in your life, that's what you attract. In his book *As a Man Thinketh*, James Allen stresses how important it is to think well of ourselves, because our thoughts direct the course of our lives. Allen believed that our thoughts make us who we are, and we attract what we think. So, if you think good things about yourself, and you expect them to happen, they will happen. In general, positive people make more money; a study of insurance salesmen revealed that those with the most optimistic attitudes sold 88 percent more policies than their pessimistic co-workers. They were less likely to throw in the towel when they came across obstacles on the job, and they were less likely to get frustrated and quit. Also, the optimists were hopeful about the future of their careers in the industry.

How to Focus on Positive Thoughts

Well, it's easier said than done, but it's possible; as with anything in life, the more you practice, the better you'll become at it. Here are some tips on how to switch your thinking from negative to positive.

Identify Your Self-Defeating Beliefs: Your values, attitudes, and personal views make up your belief system. Your beliefs are a part of who you are; they shape the way you see yourself and your world. When these beliefs are self-defeating, they set you up for dissatisfaction and failure. For example, if you believe that your self-worth is connected to your achievements, you will only feel fulfilled when you have reached your desired status, achieved your goals, or excelled at your career. Your self-defeating beliefs will play a role in your negative thought patterns.

Identify Negative Thought Patterns: Negative thought patterns are also referred to as cognitive distortions. They show up during times of stress and confirm your self-defeating beliefs. For example, if you believe that your self-worth is defined by your accomplishments, you will feel okay as long as you're winning, but when you are faced with unexpected obstacles or setbacks, negative thinking patterns can cause you to exaggerate or over-analyze the severity of the situation and lead to unnecessary anxiety. At this point, you might start having negative thoughts such as blaming yourself for not achieving what you were aiming for, believing you're a failure or that you'll never succeed at anything. If you keep thinking like this, it will destroy your confidence, and could lead to depression.

Your personal beliefs are learned during childhood, and they develop as you mature into adulthood. Since that's what you were raised with, that's all you know. You've accepted these beliefs as normal, and they are therefore very difficult to change. I learned my personal beliefs about money from my parents. Even though I came from a middle-class family, and my dad was an accountant, we were always broke. My mother and father were always arguing about money, their credit cards were always maxed out, and they had no savings. They would say things like, "Vacation homes are for rich people; we can't afford that." Or, if we were driving past a nice area, and one of my siblings or I said, "Oh, Mommy, that's a nice house," one of them would respond, "Well, get a good look, sweetie, because we could never afford a house like that." The statement was then reinforced by the other parent. It is no surprise that I grew up resenting wealthy people, blowing my paycheck every month and maxing out my credit cards. It took me a while to undo my negative thinking patterns, and I still practice these techniques today because it's easy to slip back into old habits.

Start with Gratitude: I've found that gratitude is one of the most powerful ways to shift your thinking. My mentor advised me to start practicing it, and I haven't looked back since. Many of the successful people we admire such as Oprah Winfrey, Tim Ferriss, John Paul DeJoria, and Richard Branson also practice gratitude. In an interview with *Business Insider*, John Paul DeJoria states that one of the most important things for him is to spend the first five minutes of his day being thankful for life. I believe, and many others agree, that being grateful for what you already have instead of focusing on your lack, makes the difference between success and failure.

Gratitude is defined as the acknowledgement and appreciation of what we have and the opportunities that are coming.

When we are thankful for the small things, bigger things show up in our lives. I once heard someone say that gratitude is the key that unlocks the door to abundance. Let's take a look at why.

Gratitude Helps Us Live in the Present: Most of us don't live in the present; we are either worrying about the future or living in a state of regret about the past. But we miss the power of the present moment when we step out of it. The present moment is filled with opportunities and blessings when we change our perspective of it. Everything seems a bit brighter when we pay attention to the present; it fills you with curiosity for the things you're surrounded by. Gratefulness fuels our inner energy.

Gratitude Produces Happiness: I was always miserable because my focus was on what I didn't have. But when I learned to be content with what I *did* have until I got what I wanted, I experienced a radical transformation to my state of mind. I felt joy because I appreciated what was in front of me. Happiness is not a destination; it's a choice that comes from one location— and that is within. For happiness to become your reality, you've got to focus on the things that will make you happy.

Gratitude Connects People: Showing gratitude towards our friends, family members, loved ones, colleagues, and the people we interact with on a day-to-day basis is a powerful way to connect with and influence those around us. We all have a basic human need to feel appreciated. You will often hear couples who are having troubles in their relationship say that their significant other doesn't appreciate them. When we show gratitude for the things that people do for us, it makes them feel appreciated and encourages them to continue their good work. Grateful people make wonderful friends and lovers; they are empathetic, less selfish, and more giving. In general, they love people, and that brings everyone closer together. In a world where self-seeking is the order of the day, when you are a person who freely acknowledges others' efforts, you will find that people want to be on your team.

Gratitude Is Good for the Brain: Several studies have found that gratitude strengthens the brain. A study reported in *Medical Daily* found that participants who practiced gratitude for eight weeks had a stronger brain structure for empathy, social cognition, and the area of the brain that processes reward. Brain-imaging studies have found that when we feel grateful, the brain's reward center lights up.

Gratitude Improves Our Health: Research suggests that an attitude of gratitude improves both physical and psychological health. Grateful people are more resilient when life takes a turn for the worse. They are happy with what they've got—and are likely to recover faster from illness, sleep better, and nurture their physical body. When we are grateful for what we have, we want to take care of it better.

Gratitude Eliminates Stress: A study conducted in 2017 and published in *Scientific Reports* discovered that heart rates decreased amongst the participants who practiced gratitude. One of the effects of stress is an elevated heart rate, which contributes to overwhelm and anxiety. The more you think about the problems that are causing stress in your life, the faster your heart beats, and the worse the anxiety and overwhelm become. One of the reasons gratitude reduces the heart rate is that your thoughts are now centered on something peaceful, and this helps you relax. The next time you're feeling stressed and overwhelmed, start practicing gratitude, and your entire disposition will change. It's not the easiest thing to do, but it's definitely possible.

It Builds Resilience: Mental resilience is one of the most important survival mechanisms for human beings. When the mind is strong, your circumstances can't define you. A strong mind gives you the ability to see the calm after the storm, when you're still in the storm. It's a faith builder; you have this inner knowing that even though your situation looks nothing like your desired outcome, better days are ahead of you. In 2006, the *Behavior Research and Therapy* journal published a study that found that veterans who practiced gratitude had lower rates of post-traumatic stress disorder. Veterans are respected not just because they fought for our country, but because they've been exposed to horrors that the average person will never encounter. Despite the hell they've been through, some of them still manage to become productive members of society after service. As the study highlighted, one of the reasons for this is that they practice gratitude, which helps them to zoom out of their bad experiences and focus on the good ones.

HOW TO PRACTICE GRATITUDE

I practice gratitude twice a day. It's the first thing I do when I wake up in the morning, and the last thing I do before I go to sleep at night. I keep a gratitude journal and a pen on my bedside table. I write down three things that I'm grateful for, and I focus on the feeling of gratitude. If you find that difficult, just think about how you feel when someone gives you a present that you like. It's that warm, fuzzy feeling that makes you hug the person and say thank you. Once you get that feeling, focus on it for five minutes. I find that it helps to keep saying thank you for the three things I've written down.

Practice Laughter Therapy: Laughter is medicine to the soul. Research has found that, as well as helping you see things in a positive light, laughing has several benefits. Here are some of them:

- **Relaxes the Body:** Laughter triggers muscle relaxation and circulation, both of which help to relieve some of the physical symptoms associated with stress.

- **Stimulates the Organs:** Laughter increases your oxygen intake which stimulates the muscles, lungs, and heart.

- **Improves Mood:** Laughter helps you focus on positive thoughts because it improves your mood. Laughter feels good because it triggers the release of endorphins, the feel-good hormones. Laugher helps reduce feelings of anxiety and depression.

- **Provides Pain Relief:** Endorphins are also the body's natural pain reliever.

- **Strengthens the Immune System:** Negative thoughts trigger the release of stress hormones such as cortisol and adrenaline. When these chemicals are present in the body longer than they need to be, they weaken the immune system. But laughter triggers the release of neuropeptides, which help fight stress and illness.

I have practiced laugher therapy for many years, and I can say with confidence that it's a powerful way to eliminate negative thinking. You can induce laughter by watching your favorite comedian, reading some jokes, or anything else that you find funny.

Practice Positive Self-Talk: Whether out loud or inwardly, self-talk is the conversation we have with ourselves—and it can be either good or bad. Positive self-talk will motivate and encourage you, but negative self-talk will limit you. Here are some tips on how to practice positive self-talk:

- **Stop the Comparison Game:** Comparison was something I used to struggle with. I would compare myself to everyone—friends, family members, and co-workers. If I felt I didn't measure up, I'd get depressed and start negative self-talk. Unfortunately, we live in a world that encourages us to be dissatisfied with ourselves. Turn on the television or flick through a magazine, and we're bombarded with images of what we're supposed to look like, the car we should drive, the type of partner we should have on our arm, and so on and so on. We are told how we should look and what we should own in order to feel satisfied with life, and if we fall short, or the people around us have these things, we feel insecure. But you can stop comparing yourself to others by setting your own standards and conforming to them only. Define success for yourself and strive for that. Instead of comparing yourself to other people, compare yourself to *yourself*. The only person you should be competing against is *you*. Also, there's no point in comparing yourself to other people—because you don't know the full story. From the outside looking in, it can appear as if some people are very successful, but the only reason they have what they have is that they've got a ton of debt. I know this to be true because that's how *I* used to live. I'm sure there were people looking at me and thinking I was living the life with the house I lived in and the car I drove—but I was broke and in debt.

- **Have Positive Conversations:** If you pay attention to the conversations that people have, you will notice they are typically very negative. Just sit at the bus stop, go to a restaurant, or eavesdrop on the conversations your work colleagues have. We're either complaining about the bad weather, our boss, relationship issues, or some other problem. Positive conversations are rare, and when you hear them, it sounds strange because that's not what you're used to hearing. It's easy to get sucked into negative conversations because the reality is that we live in a vicious world. From the senseless killings, to war, and corrupt governmental affairs, we are surrounded by negativity. But instead of participating, why not steer the conversation in another direction and speak about something positive? As I've mentioned, I was once the naysayer—I had a problem for every solution, and I'd shut down anyone who tried to put a positive spin on a conversation. I was so miserable that I couldn't stand to be around positive people. I didn't understand why they were so happy—didn't things ever go wrong in their lives? Anyway, here's an example of turning a negative conversation into a positive one:

Simon: "Oh my goodness, I'm so tired of this weather; it rains all the time."

You: "For some people, rain is a blessing; take farmers, for example—if it doesn't rain, their crops won't grow, and they can't make an income."

Simon: "You're right. I never thought about it like that."

The aim is to spend the majority of your time in a positive frame of mind, whether you're alone or with other people.

Positive Affirmations: I found positive affirmations very helpful when I first started my journey of building better habits. I started and ended my day with them, and they really helped me get into the habit of speaking kindly to myself. I also wrote them down on note cards and repeated them several times throughout the day. Here are some of my favorites:

- I am capable of achieving every goal I have set for myself.
- I am more than enough.
- I am an overcomer.
- My fears have no power over me.
- I am in charge of my destiny.
- I won't compare myself to anyone because I am confident in who I am.
- I hold the keys to transforming my life.

- **Let Go of the Past:** One of the biggest energy drainers of all time is focusing on the past. It's a pointless endeavor because if there is one thing in the world we can't do, it's go back in time. No scientist or engineer has designed a time capsule yet, so we can't go back to last week, last month, or last year and change our actions. We made the mistake, we said the wrong thing, we were careless with money—whatever it was, learn from it and move on. The one thing you *can* control, though, is your future, and you should be putting all your time and energy into building the future you know you deserve.

- **Visualize Your Success:** The mind is more powerful than we can imagine. In his book *The 7 Habits of Highly Effective People*, Stephen Covey mentions an experiment that took place in the 1980s. Male participants were divided into three groups. One was told to practice playing basketball every day for a week; the second group was told not to practice; and the third group was told to visualize practicing and winning basketball for 20 minutes every day for one week. At the end of the week, they were all asked to play a basketball match. Which group do you think won? The group who visualized playing and winning. Why is that? Because the brain is so powerful that when you imagine moving a certain part of your body, it trains the muscles just as much as if you were actually performing the movement. Basically, when you focus your mind on something with great intensity and the corresponding emotion, it becomes your reality.

  Spend ten minutes every day visualizing your success. I find that visualization is most effective when I listen to calming music—you can find some on You-Tube. Start by sitting or lying in a comfortable position.

Close your eyes and relax by taking some deep breaths. Focus on what you want to achieve as if you've already achieved it. Imagine what it feels like, what it looks like, what it smells like, sounds like, and tastes like. Imagine how you would *feel* living your dream life.

- **Thought Replacement:** Thought replacement is a technique used in cognitive behavioral therapy to get people to change the way they think. It's another difficult strategy, but it works if you're diligent. One of the reasons it's difficult is that the majority of our thoughts take place on a subconscious level; we don't think about what we're thinking about. Experts suggest that we have approximately 6,000 thoughts per day. Now, that's a lot of thoughts, right? So, there's no way we can monitor all of them. But we *can* monitor the ones we catch. Thought replacement is similar to positive self-talk except you only do it when you catch yourself thinking a negative thought. Let's say you catch yourself thinking, "I'm so dumb; I can't believe I didn't know the answer to that question." Replace that thought with something like, "I am extremely intelligent; it's perfectly normal not to know the answer to every question."

- **Spend Time with Optimists:** Positive people will force you to think like them because they won't tolerate your negativity. If you're serious about changing the way you think, get around some optimists, and they'll have a very positive influence on you. When my mentality started shifting, I made a point of seeking out people who were on the same frequency as me. Although most of my friends ditched me, I found it difficult to keep company with the ones who stayed. I ended up ditching them because I was trying to live out this new life, but they weren't ready to make the change. I kept trying to talk about all this amazing stuff I'd been learning, but they didn't take me seriously, and they had no interest in it. Although I hadn't made a complete change, I had to get around people who believed in the same principles as me. I found my tribe through my mentor; he introduced me to some amazing people, and their energy was infectious. There was no atmosphere of doom and gloom; they spoke about their ideas, goals, and how they could make other people's dreams become a reality. For a long time, I just sat, listened, and drank in all their wisdom. It was a very fruitful time in my life; there was no room for negativity with them.

- **Practice Cognitive Reframing:** Cognitive reframing is a technique used in psychology to change a person's perspective about a relationship, person, or situation. It's similar to thought replacement, but slightly different. The main idea behind reframing is that the frame through which someone looks at their situation determines how they perceive it. When the frame is moved, the meaning changes, and the thoughts and behavior follow. Another way of understanding reframing is to think about looking through a camera lens frame. You can change the look of the picture by altering the lens; you can view it so that it's further away or closer. It's the same picture, but it's seen differently.

  Cognitive reframing teaches you to change the way you look at a problem by asking yourself questions such as "Are there any other reasons why this has happened?" or "How else can I look at this situation?" Coming up with alternatives may stop you from overreacting about the situation. It's also important to mention that cognitive reframing isn't about invalidating or denying your feelings—it's about acknowledging how you feel while at the same time thinking about different reasons. For example, say you've just started dating a guy/girl. They've been calling, texting, and liking all your posts on social media—and they suddenly stop. Your first thought is that they've met someone else and that's who they're giving all their attention to now. Or you assume you said something off-putting in your last conversation, and now they're not interested. Reframing the situation would involve acknowledging you're concerned about why they've stopped contacting you while reminding yourself that neither of you signed a contract stating you must contact each other every day. They might be busy with work, there might be a family emergency, or they might have lost their phone. These are all legitimate reasons why you may not have heard from your new date.

As I've stated several times throughout this book, your mind is your most valuable asset, and it will steer your life in the direction you want it to go in if you are disciplined enough to change your thoughts. I can now say with confidence that you *are* what you think—and you will become exactly what you focus on...

Speaking of thinking, now it's time to consider your environment. Just as I was, you'll be shocked to discover that an untidy home can be a breeding ground for failure! In Chapter 4, I'll teach you all about it.

CHAPTER 4:

ENVIRONMENT IS EVERYTHING

The first time my mentor came to my house, he was horrified. He did a walk-through, told me he'd call me later—and left. I stood staring at the front door for about five minutes, bewildered at what had just happened. Mike had asked to come over to my place for a coffee so we could go over some stuff. I was really looking forward to spending time with him, asking questions and getting to know more about how he became successful. After I had got over the initial shock, I pulled my tie off and flung it around the banister, kicked my shoes off into opposite ends of the room and made my way into the kitchen to see if I could find a clean plate to eat the rest of my pizza on.

Mike did call later that evening as promised, and the first thing he said to me was, "Buddy, if you want to be successful, you've got to tidy up your house. And I don't mean just make things look neat on the surface—you need to declutter completely and turn your home into a sanctuary." He went on to give me scientific facts about how an untidy environment can have a negative effect on your state of mind (I'll talk about that in a bit). Mike said he'd been just like me at my age, and it wasn't until he got organized that his life started to change. I knew he was right because I only had to remember how I'd felt when I'd gone to his house in comparison to how I felt when I was at home. I felt like Superman when I was at Mike's, and when I got home, I felt as if it would never be possible to reach my goals. I'd assumed it was because I was in the presence of a successful person, which made the idea of success more tangible for me. But the problem was my environment. Let's take a look at why an untidy home has the ability to hinder your progress.

Clutter Causes Stress: Are you surprised? What's it like trying to look for something when your house is a mess? Stressful. I remember the days when I was late for work because I couldn't find my car keys. My keys would always land wherever they landed, and the next morning, I'd get all flustered trying to look for them. One study reported that people who referred to their homes as cluttered and full of unfinished projects were more tired, depressed, and had excess cortisol in their bloodstream in comparison to those who described their homes as "restorative" and "restful." The study also reported that high levels of cortisol can accelerate disease and cause chronic stress.

Clutter Interferes with Your Diet: Who wants to cook in a kitchen full of dirty dishes? I know I didn't, and so instead of making a healthy meal at home, I would go out to eat. For breakfast I'd grab a McDonald's, and for lunch it was pizza. Research has found that people make healthier food choices when they are in an orderly environment. One of the reasons for this is that, as mentioned, clutter causes stress, which leads to coping mechanisms such as overeating and comfort foods.

Clutter Affects Your Breathing: I had severe allergies when my house was cluttered; my nose was always running, and my eyes were always itching. I didn't know why until I read that cluttered homes gather more dust and attract dust mites, which can lead to breathing problems and allergies.

Clutter Affects Your Relationships: According to research, hoarders have higher rates of divorce. This is especially true when one partner is not a hoarder; when spouses are forced to live in such environments, they express their discomfort through negative comments, judgment, name-calling, irritability, and anger. Although I wouldn't call myself a hoarder, I was very untidy, and that was one of the reasons I could never keep a girlfriend. She either got fed up of cleaning up my mess, or she'd refuse to come round altogether.

Clutter Isolates You: This was never my problem as I was completely shameless about the mess in my house. My excuse was, "I'm a man—I'm supposed to be untidy." But one survey found that almost half of the homeowners interviewed said they wouldn't invite friends over when their house was untidy.

Clutter Will Block Your Promotion: A study conducted by CareerBuilder discovered that 28 percent of employers would not promote an employee with an untidy desk.

Clutter Limits Productivity: A cluttered environment makes it difficult to focus; I definitely struggled with this when I started my course. I thought I was distracted because I was on the phone all the time, but that wasn't the case. It was the mess causing the distraction, and that led me to reach for the phone to distract myself from the mess. The Princeton University Neuroscience Institute conducted a study and found that when there are too many things on your desk, the brain becomes more focused on the items than the task you are trying to complete. The study also found that a tidy work environment increases your productivity levels, improves your ability to process information, and makes you less moody.

The verdict is in! Clutter is a hindrance to your progress. So, what are you waiting for? Get decluttering!

HOW TO CLEANSE YOUR HOME OF NEGATIVE ENERGY

Now that you've cleaned out the physical clutter from your home, it's time to get rid of the negative energy that's been left behind. Everything is energy—that pile of clothes, paperwork, and ten-year-old boots you had stashed in the back of your closet have left a trail of negative energy that you will need to get rid of. I thought I'd hit the jackpot when I finished decluttering my house, and I proudly invited Mike over for a coffee. But he did the same thing—did a walk-through, told me he'd call me later, and left! I was mortified. What was the problem *now*? Had I not cleaned up to his standards? I waited patiently for his call, and that evening he taught me all about cleansing the home of negative energy. I didn't waste any time; I got straight to work. And I can say with confidence that it is one of the most powerful habits I've acquired to date! It's also important to mention that this is not a onetime event—I've made a habit of doing it once a week. Additionally, there are also certain times when it's essential to rid your home of negative energy. These include:

- **After an Illness:** Whatever ailment you're suffering from carries negative energy; also, you will generate negative energy from the stress of not feeling well.

- **When You Feel Stuck:** Stagnation is often a sign of negative energy.

- **A Major Life Transition:** Clearing out the old energy makes space for the new energy to come in.

- **After an Argument:** Whether you've had an argument with your friend, partner, or roommate over the phone or in the home, words have power. During a heated argument, people say some mean things, and words stay in the air.

- **After a Loss or a Breakup:** A clear-out during times of grief or heartache will help with the healing process and enable you to move forward.

- **When You've Had a Bad Day:** If there's negative energy in the home and you've had a bad day, that negative energy will feed off you, and you'll stay in a bad mood.

NEGATIVE ENERGY CLEANSING TIPS

I've tried all of the tips I'm about to mention. I've found that burning dried herbs (sage) works best for me, but I had to go through all the following techniques to find that out, and I suggest you do the same:

- **Salt Cleansing:** Salt has been used as a cleansing agent for centuries. It works well on wounds, household appliances, and food, but what a lot of people are not aware of is that it also gets rid of negative energy. You can do one of the following:

  - Put a Himalayan salt lamp in each room.
  - Add salt to the water when cleaning floors and surfaces.
  - Place a small dish of salt on a table in each room.

- Sprinkle a thin layer of salt around the perimeter of your home, or at each door.
- Fill a spray bottle with salt water and spray it in each room.

• **Use Lemon as a Scent:** Have you noticed that a lot of cleaning products are lemon scented? That's because the smell of lemon is naturally uplifting and invigorating. Here are a few ways you can use it in the home:

- Add lemon essential oil to your diffuser.
- Add drops of lemon essential oil to rugs or carpets.
- Boil lemon peels and allow the scent to flow through your home.

• **Burn Incense:** Palo Santo is a powerful fragrant wood that originates from South America. It is known for its vigorous energy-cleansing properties. You can burn the stick in the same way you would incense.

• **Make Noise:** This one sounded strange to me too, but it works. The sound of gongs, drums, or the clapping of hands can get rid of negative energy. Start at your front door and move clockwise around your home making noise until you get back to the front door.

• **Crystals:** Crystals help to raise vibrations. Hematite and black tourmaline are two types of crystal you can place around your home to break up negative energy.

• **Burn Dried Herbs:** Burning dried herbs is another ancient energy-cleansing practice. Place the herbs of your choice in a firesafe container, light them, and once a flame starts burning, blow it out. The herbs will keep burning slowly while letting off smoke. Walk through your home holding the container. Here is a list of herbs you can use:

- Sage
- Sandalwood
- Tibetan monastery incense
- Juniper
- Mugwort
- Rosemary
- Yerba santa
- Cedar.

Now that you've cleansed your home, it's time to make some changes to your social circle. Keep reading to find out why.

CHAPTER 5:

YOU MIGHT NEED TO CHANGE YOUR FRIENDS

My mentor is like a well of wisdom. Everything he has told me so far has been right on the money. I am so grateful that I had him to guide me when I started out on my success journey, because I doubt I would have made it otherwise. And one of the main reasons for this would have been because of my friends. One of the first pieces of advice he gave me was to prepare myself to either lose friends, or find the strength to cut them off. This is because we are who we associate with. When I was growing up, my mom and dad would always say, "Show me your friend, and I'll show you your character." They said this anytime I brought a friend home whom they felt was going to be a bad influence on me. I found this highly annoying, but I later understood what they were saying. I used to think I was responsible for the decisions I made, and that I wasn't influenced by my friends. But when I took the time out to evaluate my life, I realized that this wasn't the case; my friends had a major influence on everything I did. Additionally, there's plenty of research suggesting that we tend to adopt the habits of the people we're psychologically and physically closest to. It's referred to as *mirroring*, and the idea is that, on an unconscious level, we emulate the traits of our friends.

If you want to test this out, take a trip to your local mall over the weekend and pay attention to a group of teenagers. You'll notice that you can't really tell them apart; they wear similar shoes and clothes, they dye their hair the same color, they talk and walk the same. As adults, the influence our friends have over us is not as obvious. In most cases, once we move into adulthood, we stop dressing the same and stop dying our hair the same color as each other. But this doesn't mean we don't take on other traits. In my situation, my friends were making me poor. I had a mountain of debt, and my spending was out of control. Is it a coincidence that we were all in the same boat? Here are three ways my friends were keeping me in a state of financial lack, and why yours might be too:

Some Friends Are Freeloaders: "Hey, can I borrow $500 to cover rent? I'll pay you back at the end of the month." The end of the month comes and goes, and no mention is made of the $500! "Oh, shoot, I forgot my wallet. Can you get this round of drinks and I'll transfer the funds over to your account?" That transfer never happens! "I really want to go on this vacation with you guys, but I had to help with my sister's school fees last month and I'm a little short. Can you put the deposit down for me and I'll pay you back before we go?" Then comes the excuse a couple of weeks before the vacation! Can you relate to any of these? Some of my friends were always asking me to lend them money, and I never got it back. One of the reasons for this was that I was a people pleaser, and I didn't like conflict, so I'd just hope they'd remember—and, conveniently, they never did. The freeloaders in the group took full advantage of this. I am in no way saying you should stop helping your friends when they're in need, but if there's a pattern, you've got a problem on your hands, and you'll need to start thinking about whether you really need friends like this.

Bad Financial Habits: "Stay for another round. We've all got to go to work tomorrow anyway; we can nurse each other's hangovers in the office." "Just put down one more bet—I've got a feeling your luck will change." These were the responses I'd get when I was out with friends and I'd say I wanted to call it a night. Again, there's nothing wrong with drinking and gambling in moderation, but my friends took it too far. We would drink and gamble until our bank accounts were empty or we'd maxed out our credit cards.

Keeping Up Appearances: When one of our friends got a new car, kitchen, or driveway, we all got one, whether we could afford it or not. I found it highly annoying that every time I got something new, so did everyone else. But I did the same thing! How hypocritical is that? I didn't want to appear as if I wasn't doing as well as everyone else. But the joke is that we all knew we were fronting. None of us could afford the lifestyles we were living. It's normal to want what those closest to us have; it's a part of the human condition. The theory of relative deprivation gives us more insight into this and suggests that when we don't have as much as the people in our inner circle, it makes us feel bad. Have you ever noticed that you're content with what you've got until a friend turns up with something better? For example, you've just bought yourself a five-year-old used car. But a week later, your best friend rolls up in a brand-new BMW fresh off the dealer's lot! Now you feel like crap and want a better car. This became a problem for me because I was always trying to keep up with my friends even though I couldn't afford it.

WHY YOUR FRIENDS ARE KEEPING YOU STUCK

Change requires discipline, and that means you've got to make sacrifices. One of the first things I did when I decided I wanted to turn my life around was take a financial management course. I was terrible with money, and I wanted to learn how to control it instead of it controlling me. It was an online course, and I studied in the evenings after work. The first thing I noticed was that my friends were not very supportive; they basically laughed at me when I told them about the course. Second, as I mentioned earlier, a three-month course took me over a year to complete because I was more committed to my friends than I was to my personal growth. I answered my phone anytime it rang or I got a message, and by the time I was done talking, I had no energy to study. What I was experiencing is known as the "crabs in the bucket" mentality. Let me give you a bit of insight into this phenomenon:

The "Crabs in the Bucket" Mentality: One crab can find its way out of a bucket. By any means necessary, it will claw its way up and return to its natural habitat. But when a bunch of crabs are in a bucket, if one of them tries to climb out, the others will pull it back down. When the crab tries again, the other crabs will go as far as to break its claws to prevent it from escaping. Ultimately, none of the crabs will ever get out because they are all working against each other. This crablike behavior is also found in humans. It's a metaphor for how some humans respond when someone in their social circle starts working on their personal development. In most cases, humans won't go as far as to physically harm someone to prevent them from achieving, but they will attempt to break their spirit when they see that someone close to them is on their way to success. This behavior takes place on a conscious or a subconscious level, and they will do whatever they can to hinder the person's progress. Success makes some people feel uncomfortable; when a friend starts winning, they feel as if they're losing. To make themselves feel better, they'll try and bring them back down to their level.

We've all heard of the saying, "Misery loves company." This is another way of looking at the "crabs in the bucket" mentality. Miserable people want to be around other miserable people because they enjoy wallowing in self-pity. There are several ways this "crabs in the bucket" mentality will manifest, and it may be different for you, but I can guarantee that it will happen. All my friends were bad with money. We had decent jobs, none of us earning less than 100K per year, but we spent everything we earned and lived off credit. None of us had any disposable income at the end of the month. We ate out several times a week, we spent hundreds of dollars every weekend partying, and we took two expensive vacations a year. One of the first things I learned on my financial management course was to write out a list of all my expenses and cut down on all unnecessary spending. I was amazed to find that I spent over half my salary on partying, eating out, and vacations. My first step was to start declining invites—and that was met by laughter and ridicule: "Oh, come on, life's too short—you need to live a little." "Wow, you've become really boring now." My favorite was, "So you think you're better than us now?" It was so frustrating. Sometimes I gave in; other times I didn't. But the more I applied what I was learning, the more my friends started distancing themselves from me. I didn't need to ditch my friends—*they* ditched *me*.

They Don't Want To Put the Work In: Breaking bad habits takes a conscious and determined effort. It means you'll need to say *no* more than you'll say *yes*, and to the people who don't understand the amount of work required to make these changes, you'll make it easy for them to drag you down to their level. Think about it like this: imagine standing on top of a table. Your friends are on the ground and you're trying to pull them up to your level. Unless you've got superhuman strength, this is going to be impossible—they'll pull you down quicker than you can pull them up. It won't be intentional, but it won't be long before they've pulled you back down to their level. Remember, it's human nature to take the path of least resistance, so when your friends keep telling you to take a break and have some fun, eventually you'll cave in, and before you know it, you'll be right back to square one.

As the saying goes, "Out with the old, in with the new." After getting rid of some of your friends, you'll need some replacements, but not in the way you think... Find out more in Chapter 6.

CHAPTER 6:

YOU WILL NEED AN ACCOUNTABILITY PARTNER

N o, you don't need new friends—you need an accountability partner. Someone who has achieved the level of success you're aiming for and who knows exactly how to get you where you need to go. An accountability partner will keep you on track and ensure you are doing what you need to do to achieve your goals. Getting an accountability partner (his name is Mike) was one of the best things I've ever done. Here's why:

They Help You Reach Your Full Potential: An accountability partner is like a personal trainer; they know how to push you past your perceived limits. I got a personal trainer before an accountability partner because I knew I wasn't pushing myself hard enough at the gym. I wanted to achieve my ideal body, but it wasn't going to happen if I kept giving up every time I got tired. Also, they could show me how to get the best use out of the gym equipment I was using. I worked out by myself for seven months before I got a personal trainer. During those seven months, I didn't see that much improvement. It took me three months to reach my body goals once I hired a trainer.

An accountability partner will highlight the areas in your life where you can make more progress. Where you think you've mastered your gift, they'll challenge your abilities and force you to improve. I don't believe there's any such thing as reaching the top of your game because there's always room for improvement. That's why athletes are always challenging themselves to beat their own record—because it's possible. But the reality is that if someone isn't overseeing that challenge, you won't have enough drive to see it through.

They Are Not Haters: The good thing about an accountability partner is that they're already way ahead of you in terms of success, and so they've got no reason to feel insecure when *you* make it. Some of your friends, on the other hand, are not going to be so happy for you when you achieve an important milestone. This is especially true if they're not there yet. Your accountability partner has walked with you on your journey, they've seen how hard you've worked—and when you succeed, they're just as happy for you as you are for yourself. Also, they took on the role because they have a passion for helping others reach their full potential. They can give you better insight into your progress and motivate you to continue moving forwards. When you are working towards achieving something, you should celebrate every small milestone—and what better person to celebrate them with than the one who is truly rooting for you?

They Keep You Motivated: Much like a personal trainer, who will demand that you do an extra 20 push-ups because they know you're not finished yet, an accountability partner will keep reminding you of your "why" so you don't quit prematurely.

Sometimes, it's difficult to motivate yourself, especially when things start going wrong. But an accountability partner has likely made the same mistakes, if not worse, and pulled through. They will remind you of their failures along their journey, what they learned from them, and how those failures shaped them into the person they are today.

Before you get an accountability partner, you need to take personal accountability for your life. It's not uncommon to believe that successful people only got to where they are today because they were born with a silver spoon in their mouth. As you will read in a moment, that is certainly not the case. The wealthy are also targets of vicious attacks from the middle and lower classes. Apparently, they are selfish and greedy and need to share what they have. In recent months, Bill Gates has been under fire for paying less tax than ordinary workers. But what people conveniently forget is that Bill Gates has probably donated more money to charity than half the inhabitants of the world put together! The bottom line is that it takes hard work and discipline to succeed in life. Even if you come from a rich family and your dad gave you the money to start a successful company, you need the discipline to maintain it. Now, I'm not even preaching to the masses here—my friends and I were always hating on successful people. Although we were relatively well off ourselves, none of us were millionaires, and we had every excuse under the sun for why we were incapable of acquiring the kind of wealth we desired—and the main one was that we didn't come from rich families.

The late preacher Dr. Myles Munroe once said that the wealthiest place in the world wasn't Kuwait, Singapore, Luxembourg, or Qatar, but the graveyard! This is one of the most profound statements I've ever heard because it's so true. We all have ambitions, dreams, and goals, but it's our responsibility to give them life—if not, we take them to the grave with us. I shudder to think how many businesses were never started, how many songs were never written, or how many basketball players never got to play in the NBA because these people died without reaching their full potential. My father spent his life talking about becoming a *New York Times* Bestseller; he was Agatha Christie's biggest critic and believed his writing capability was far superior. It may well have been, but he didn't have the discipline to turn his dream into his reality. He died in 2015 from a massive heart attack, and, like millions of other people around the world, his dream was buried with him.

There are many reasons people don't succeed in life. I am guessing that limiting self-beliefs are somewhere towards the top of the list, but I would argue that a lack of discipline is at the very top. Successful people get to the top of their game because they've mastered the art of self-discipline, and not because of the families they were born into. Life isn't about the hand you were dealt, but how you choose to play that hand. Let's take a look at the lives of some of the most successful people in the world who might never have achieved anything if they had allowed their circumstances to define them.

Ursula Burns – CEO of Xerox: Raised by a single mother in a New York City housing project, Ursula Burns could have very easily ended up a statistic, but she chose a different route. After graduating high school, she went on to study Mechanical Engineering at NYU Polytechnic School of Engineering. Burns then gained a Master's degree in Mechanical Engineering from Columbia University. At the age of 22, she was hired as an intern for Xerox. Once she had completed her degree, Ursula was hired as a full-time employee. She became the executive assistant and was later promoted to the vice president for global manufacturing. In 2009, Ursula Burns became the CEO of Xerox. She is also on the board of directors of several companies including American Express Corporation, Exxon Mobil Corporation, and Datto Inc. Burns also provides leadership counsel to non-profit organizations and was appointed by Barack Obama as the vice chair of the President's Export Council. *Forbes* has several times given her the accolade of one the 100 most powerful women in the world.

Leslie "Les" Brown – Motivational Speaker: Les Brown is probably my favorite person on this list. I've been listening to him for years; his story is just so inspiring. Les Calvin Brown is a twin. He and his brother were born in one of the most dangerous areas in Miami—Liberty City. Their mother gave birth to them on the floor of an abandoned building. She was married to a soldier who had been deployed, so when she got pregnant from another man, she was forced to give the children up for adoption to prevent her husband from finding out. Les Brown and his brother were adopted at six weeks of age by Mamie Brown, a 38-year-old domestic cleaner and cafeteria cook.

His adoptive mother was terribly poor, but Brown and his brother were loved unconditionally. He credits his success to the confidence Mamie Brown had in him. She always believed her son would one day become somebody great, despite his disabilities. In the fifth grade, he was labeled "educable mentally retarded." He didn't do very well in high school, and his teachers didn't believe he would ever amount to anything. Unfortunately, he accepted the label he had been given, and he suffered from low self-esteem.

In many of his speeches, Brown talks about one of the defining moments in his life. He was asked by a speech and drama instructor called LeRoy Washington to write something on the blackboard. Les responded to the teacher saying that he wasn't able to do it because he was educable mentally retarded. Washington told Brown never to refer to himself like that again, and to go ahead and write on the blackboard because he had the ability to do anything he put his mind to. It was at this moment that his life changed—because he started to believe that he really could achieve anything he put his mind to.

Les Brown just managed to graduate from high school, but he didn't go to college because he was determined to fulfil his lifelong dream of becoming a disc jockey. After much perseverance, he was eventually hired by one of the most prominent radio stations in the United States. Unfortunately, due to his controversial topics of conversation and his refusal to apologize for the things he said that listeners found offensive, he was fired. But losing his job ended up being a blessing in disguise, and his mentor at the time, Mike Williams, who saw his great potential to become an international speaker, encouraged him to run for the Ohio Legislature. He won.

In the 1980s, he started working as a motivational speaker. All he had was a suitcase of clothes and a tape of his speeches. He couldn't afford an apartment, so he rented an office, slept on the floor, and washed in the bathroom sink. Les Brown spent his time reading books and studying the most successful motivational speakers. He started off speaking to grade-school students, and within four years, he had been awarded the National Speakers Association's Council of Peers Award of Excellence. Today, Les Brown is known as one of the most impactful motivational speakers in the world.

Andrew Carnegie – Steel Tycoon: Andrew Carnegie was born and raised in Scotland. He was the son of a poor hand-loom weaver, and he was raised in terrible poverty. His most prominent childhood memories are of sleeping to rid himself of hunger pains. At the age of 13, his family moved to America. To help with the bills, Carnegie worked for 12 hours a day, six days a week as a bobbin boy, changing thread in a cotton mill. He went on to work as a messenger boy for *The Telegraph* and got promoted to an operator.

Carnegie loved to read, and every Saturday, he was given access to the personal library of Colonel James Anderson. It was during this time that he learned the information that would eventually help him turn his life around. He later went to work on the railroads and became very familiar with the transport industry. His business acumen also grew substantially; he started investing in steel and made his money back tenfold.

By 1889, he was the owner of Carnegie Steel Corporation, which became the largest steel company in the world. He was bought out by JP Morgan in 1901 for $480 million and then went on to establish several foundations including the Carnegie Mellon University. When Andrew Carnegie died in 1919, he was known as a generous philanthropist and the richest man in the world.

Kenny Troutt – Founder of Excel: Kenny Troutt came from a poor family; his father was a bartender, and Kenny was forced to work from a young age to help sustain the household. Desperate to get out of the cycle of poverty, he managed to finish school and go to college, where he paid his fees by selling insurance. After graduation, he co-founded Excel with his business partner Steve Smith. Within nine years, the company had earned billions of dollars in revenue, and Excel became the fastest-growing company in the United States.

Lakshmi Mittal – Steel Tycoon: Lakshmi Mittal is the CEO and chair of the steel company ArcelorMittal. He is one of the world's most successful billionaires and has helped put the steel industry on the global map. He was raised in a poor Indian family; the first years of his life were spent living with his extended family in a house built by his grandfather. He slept on beds made from rope, and hard floors. His father scraped enough money together to move to Calcutta and start a steel business where Mittal was employed after graduating from college. It was here that he learned about the steel industry, and later went on to start his own company. Reports suggest that he is now worth more than $12 billion.

Leonardo Del Vecchio – Italian Businessman: After his father died, Leonardo's mother was forced to put him in an orphanage because she couldn't afford to look after him and her other four children. He was later employed by a factory that made eyeglass frames and molds of auto parts. Del Vecchio opened his own molding shop at the age of 23. His company eventually became the largest maker of sunglasses and prescription eyewear including Oakley and Ray-Ban.

I think you get my point. Now, go ahead and take personal accountability for *your* life, and then get yourself an accountability partner to help take you to the next level. As you've read, there are plenty of people who have succeeded, despite not having the best start in life. Your level of success isn't dependent upon your circumstances—it's a mindset that you need to cultivate. The Les Browns and Leonardo Del Vecchios of this world could have used their upbringing as an excuse for failure, but instead, they chose to drop the victim mentality and use their adversity as a stepping stone for greatness—and you can too. If you're still making excuses for why you haven't achieved your goals, it's probably because you've adopted a victim mentality. In Chapter 7, I'll teach you how to free yourself from this mentality that's keeping you bound.

CHAPTER 7:

FREE YOURSELF FROM THE VICTIM MENTALITY

L ife sucks sometimes. The majority of people will eventu ally come to this conclusion. But as you've just read, hard times don't mean you can't succeed. Unfortunately, no matter how difficult life has been for you, no one is going to give you what you want because they feel sorry for you. Whether or not you achieve your dreams depends on the decisions *you* make. If you are going to sit and wallow in self-pity about what you've been through, expect to remain in that position. Imagine where Les Brown would be now if he had accepted his disability; the world would not have been blessed with his wisdom. The reality is that he had every right to give up, and no one would have thought any less of him. But he decided that he was going to become who he was destined to be—and so can you. Before you can free yourself from the victim mentality, you need to become familiar with its three main beliefs:

- I'm going to fail anyway so there's no point in trying.
- Everything and everyone is to blame for my misfortune.
- I always attract negative circumstances.

According to experts, people with a victim mentality don't take responsibility for their position in life. They blame everything, from their upbringing to the way they've been treated, for their inability to achieve their dreams. There are also several recognizable character traits associated with the victim mentality. These include:

A Sense of Entitlement: They have a chip on their shoulder and believe that the world owes them something because they were not born into wealth. Everyone should feel sorry for them, and they expect handouts from anyone who is capable of assisting them because of their underprivileged situation. They truly believe they have no control over the decisions they make, and neither are they responsible for the consequences associated with those actions. Personal accountability is nonexistent for the person with a victim mentality because everything that happens in their life is because of some external force that's out of their control. They can't make things happen because things just happen *to* them.

Low Self-Esteem: It's difficult to feel good about yourself when you want more out of life but can't achieve it because you believe you are the world's number one enemy. Such people don't think they're intelligent enough to earn more money, or talented enough to become successful. Because they accept their insecurities as fact, they won't invest in themselves by taking a course to improve their skills or going back to school to get the qualifications they need. They refuse to make the effort required to change their circumstances and waste their energy playing the blame game instead of using those obstacles as a stepping stone to better themselves.

Frustration, Resentment, and Anger: When you think the whole world is out to get you, including friends and family members, life becomes very frustrating. The burden of these emotions makes you see the worst in everything. You interpret innocent comments as insults, you resent anyone around you who's successful, and you feel an overall sense of anger because you've chosen to accept defeat.

Limiting Beliefs: When you've got a problem for every solution, you cause your own stagnation. The victim mentality prevents a person from moving forwards, because when an opportunity arises, they come up with ten different reasons why they can't do it. But deep down, the real reason is that they don't believe in themselves, so there's no point in trying. I was once put forward for a managerial position that would have paid double the salary I was on. I agonized over the job for weeks, thinking about all the reasons why I was unqualified for such a high-ranking position. The job was in another city, so I used that as an excuse, but the real reason was that I truly believed I wasn't good enough for the job.

Learned Helplessness: Children raised in a household where one or both parents have a victim mentality will adopt the same behavior. Children are like sponges; everything they learn comes from their immediate environment—and if that's the mentality they are exposed to from birth, there's a high chance they will grow up believing it. I think learned helplessness is the worst because as far as the individual is concerned, it's normal, they literally don't know any better because that's the only way of thinking that's been modeled to them.

Negative Self-Talk and Self-Sabotage: Everyone has a negative inner critic that attempts to stop them from achieving their goals. When you want to go on a diet, it's that voice that says, "There's no point; you don't have the willpower to see it through." Or, when you want to take a course so you can get a promotion, it's that voice that says, "Don't bother; you won't get the promotion anyway—you're up against some of the most well-respected people in the company." Most of us can override this voice and get on with it, but those with a victim mentality will embrace the voice, and that's all they listen to. Such thoughts might include:

- "No one will ever love me because I'm too ugly."
- "I never get anything right. I'm totally useless."
- "No one cares about me."
- "I deserve everything I get, so there's no point in feeling sorry for myself."

Negative self-talk leads to self-sabotage because when you tell yourself something often enough, you start to believe it, and once you believe it, you live it. People with a victim mentality live from a place of lack, and because they don't know how to talk themselves out of it, all their worst fears become their reality.

HOW TO FREE YOURSELF FROM THE VICTIM MENTALITY

This sounds like no fun at all, does it? But not to worry—it's not all doom and gloom. The fact that you're reading this book is an indication that you want more out of life. You might have some of the personality traits associated with the victim mentality, but that's okay because once upon a time, I did too—and now I don't. There are strategies you can implement to free yourself from the victim mentality. They worked for me, and I believe they'll work for you too.

Self-Compassion: Basically, don't be so hard on yourself. Think about it like this: Would you talk to your friend the way you speak to yourself? Probably not—right? When your friend lets you know that they're about to apply for a promotion, do you tell them not to bother because there's no way they're going to get it? When they confide in you that they're not happy with their weight and they want to go on a diet and start working out, do you say, "You might as well forget about it because you don't have the willpower to see it through"? No, you don't. You're going to encourage them in the best way you can. So, why not speak to yourself in the same loving way? Deep down, you know you shouldn't be speaking to yourself the way you do—which is why you'd never speak to anyone else like that. You can become more self-compassionate by changing your inner voice. It will take a while because you're so used to tuning in to the negative voice. When you start speaking kind words to yourself, it won't feel right. But persevere—because you'll get there in the end. Here's how your new conversation should go: When you catch yourself thinking, "There's no point in me applying for that job. I'm too stupid; I'll never get it," instead, say something like, "I know I'm smart enough to get this job. Getting a few extra qualifications will increase my chances of getting it. I think I'll give this a try." When you catch yourself thinking something like, "There's no way she's going to be interested in a loser like me," replace that thought with something like, "I'm an amazing person, and I deserve to be loved by someone who's equally as amazing."

Learn How to Forgive: A lot of people with a victim mentality hold a grudge against those they think have wronged them and are responsible for their failure in life. It's okay to be angry, to feel let down, to feel hurt, but there comes a time when you've got to release those feelings. You see, when you hold a grudge, the only person you're hurting is yourself. You're the one storing bitterness in your soul, and you're the one who can't move forward because you've chosen to carry a burden that doesn't belong to you. Often, the person who hurt us doesn't realize they've done so because hurt people hurt people, and the way they treated you is how they've been treated all their lives, so its normal to them. Or they just don't care—they're living their best life, while you can't sleep at night because of what they've done to you.

One of the best lessons I've ever learned about forgiveness came from Oprah Winfrey. Her mother gave birth to her when she was a teenager and wasn't able to look after her, so she sent Oprah to live with her grandmother. Oprah held terrible resentment towards her mother because of what she endured as a child. When Oprah rose to fame, her mother, whom she hadn't seen in years, returned, and she made it known to everyone who would listen that she was Oprah's mother, in the hope of gaining a profit. During an interview, she made a statement that Oprah was who she was because of the love she had given to her as a child, and she truly believed this, despite the fact she had abandoned her. To the average mind, such a statement made no sense. How could she have the audacity to make such a claim when she hadn't raised her? But Oprah put it into perspective when she said that she had to accept that her mother really wasn't delusional, but she was speaking the truth as she knew it. Her mother really did love her with everything she had; the woman had been raised in a loveless and abusive household, so she could only give Oprah what she had been given. When Oprah received this revelation, she was able to forgive her mother, as she told her on her deathbed.

Whether a person hurt you intentionally or unintentionally, your responsibility is to forgive them, regardless of the damage it has caused you. Forgiveness doesn't mean you allow that person back into your life and play happy families with them, but it does mean you've let go of all malice, bitterness, and ill feeling towards them.

Acts of Kindness: Anyone can feel sorry for themselves if they focus on what's going wrong in their lives. We get frustrated when we hear the rich and famous talk about their struggles with depression because our thought process is, "Well, what do they have to be depressed about? They've got everything they need to live happy and productive lives." Well, that's clearly not the case, because money can't buy everything; it can buy material wealth, but not spiritual wealth—and that's what humans crave more than anything else in the world. People get depressed and feel disappointed with life for many reasons, and one of them is that much of our time is spent focusing on what we don't have. The rich person might have money, but they don't have true love—and that's what keeps them up at night. Another person may have found the love of their life, but they don't have money—and that's what keeps them up at night. In other words, we can't have everything, and there's always going to be some type of lack in life. But one of the keys to happiness is to remember that there are people around you who would do anything to trade places with you. Acts of kindness involve giving what you have to those who are less fortunate than you. In this way, you stop focusing on your lack and focus on the things you *do* have, to give to others.

The victim mentality is just one of the many bad habits that will keep you stuck. Another bad habit is procrastination. You'll read all about it in Chapter 8.

CHAPTER 8:

HOW TO BEAT PROCRASTINATION

Do you have a paper to write, a project to work on, or a book to read—but instead you'd rather scroll through social media or watch a YouTube video? If so, you are no different from the average person; the majority of people would rather spend their time engaging in short-term, satisfying activities than long-term, difficult goals. Everyone struggles with procrastination. The question is *why*? You will find the answer hidden in the curse of instant gratification.

THE CURSE OF INSTANT GRATIFICATION

We live in a microwave society; we have been trained to want what we want and to get it immediately. Technology has advanced so quickly that we have access to what we need at the click of a button. In many ways this is a good thing; for example, I like having the security of an Amazon Prime membership, knowing that whatever I order will arrive in 24 hours. I like the fact that I can order food online and have it delivered to me within a few minutes. I like the fact that I can easily connect with friends and family members in different countries. I like the fact that I can access the Internet through my phone when I'm on the go. But there's also a dark side to this: immediate access to what you want encourages instant gratification.

What Is Instant Gratification?: It is the act of experiencing instant satisfaction instead of sacrificing for a future benefit. You might think there's nothing wrong with this, but research proves that it hinders your ability to become successful. Here's why.

In 1972, Stanford psychology professor Walter Mischel conducted an experiment known as the "marshmallow test." It involved leaving children between the ages of three and five alone in a room with two plates full of tasty-looking treats. The researchers told the children that they were leaving the room to do some work and that the children could eat any of the smaller treats on the plate; however, if they waited until the researcher returned, they could have one of the bigger treats. Once the door was closed, the children were monitored through a two-way mirror to see how they would deal with the temptation. The study revealed that the children who had enough self-discipline to wait for the greater reward got higher SAT scores, did better in school, had better emotional coping skills, higher self-esteem, and were less likely to abuse drugs. The children who gave in to the temptation of the early treat got low SAT scores, had low self-discipline, and were in bad health or obese in their adult life.

When we feel the desire to engage in something pleasurable, whether it's entertainment, food, or sex, rarely do we spend time processing that feeling and having a conversation with ourselves such as, "I'm feeling peckish right now. I'd love to eat that slice of chocolate cake, but I think I'll wait." Humans are wired to act on our urges as soon as we feel them because we want to indulge in a pleasurable experience. Back in the day, this worked to our advantage—our ancestors had to think and act quickly or they wouldn't survive. They rarely thought about long-term gain. Planning for the future is important, but when a predator is on your heels, or you are given the chance to eat until you are full—because starvation was a much bigger problem than obesity back then—you are going to do what is necessary to survive.

The opposite of instant gratification is delayed gratification. Why do we find it so difficult to wait for what we want? It's clear that delayed gratification is the wiser option, so why don't we choose it more often?

INSTANT GRATIFICATION THEORY

One of the most basic motivators in humans is the desire to seek pleasure and avoid pain. In psychology, this is known as the pleasure principle. The term was coined by Sigmund Freud, and it can apply to many different areas of life. Psychologist Shahram Heshmat provides several reasons why it's so difficult to choose pain instead of pleasure.

- **The Discomfort of Delay:** Self-denial is uncomfortable; the physical feeling of wanting something you can't have is something we'd rather avoid. Our instincts push us to seek out the pleasurable experience as soon as it's presented.

- **Poverty:** The need for shelter and food makes delaying gratification even more difficult. The poor person who is starving and doesn't have money for food isn't going to think about the consequences of stealing. Their main concern is satisfying their hunger, even though stealing could put their freedom at risk.

- **Anticipation:** Anticipation can influence our decision to seek immediate gratification or to delay it. The thought of the pleasurable feeling can lead us to want to indulge immediately or wait because we know the wait will make the reward even sweeter.

- **Mood:** Even people who regulate their emotions well can get thrown off track by their current mood. Everyone experiences impatience, boredom, and bad moods, all of which can entice us very quickly to indulge in what we know is not good for us.

- **Emotional Regulation:** People who find it difficult to regulate their emotions are more susceptible to instant gratification because when you're feeling down, your first instinct is to want to feel better, and you will indulge in whatever gives you that feeling without considering the consequences.

- **Impulsiveness:** Those with an impulsive, spontaneous nature find delayed gratification more difficult than others. Impulsiveness is associated with problems such as obesity and addiction.

- **Cognitive Capacity:** A forward-thinking perspective is linked to higher intelligence. Those who are naturally more intelligent are better able to consider the benefits of delayed gratification and take the appropriate action.

- **Age:** Older people have more life experiences, so they are more likely to think things through before taking action. On the other hand, younger people are a lot more impulsive and are more likely to act on their urges as soon as they feel them.

- **Uncertainty:** We are born totally dependent on our carers; we trust them, and we are certain that they will meet our needs. As we grow older, we learn that people are not as reliable as we once believed, and our futures are not as secure as we were expecting. As a result, we start to value the things we know are certain but less beneficial—such as hitting the snooze button and enjoying those few extra minutes of comfort instead of getting out of bed and going to the gym. We know the bed feels good, we are certain of that, but we don't know how long it's going to take to get the body of our dreams.

- **Imagination:** Faith plays an important role in delayed gratification. You must have the ability to see your future and believe it's possible to achieve it. When your vision is so intense you can almost feel it, you will say no to anything that creates an obstacle between you and that vision, and that includes immediate gratification.

Here are some examples of instant gratification you are probably familiar with:

- The desire to spend all your time with your new boyfriend/girlfriend instead of working on your long-term goals.

- The desire to use your credit card to book a vacation instead of saving a couple of hundred dollars a month for a year.

- The temptation to go to the bar with friends instead of going to bed early so you can wake up early and work on your goals.

- The desire to hit the snooze button and stay in bed for an extra half an hour instead of working on your side hustle.

- The urge to have a bag of chips or a chocolate bar when you're supposed to be eating healthy.

Okay, so at this point, you're probably thinking, "Well, I can kiss goodbye to having any fun in life!" Listen, there's nothing wrong with indulging in a guilty pleasure every once in a while. The problem starts when you *keep* choosing instant over delayed gratification. If this sounds like you, you're probably battling with an instant gratification bias. Keep reading to find out how to deal with this...

How to Beat the Instant Gratification Bias

Saying no to what you want is difficult, and if you're anything like me, it's going to take you a while to get over it. If it was easy, all men would have a body like Michael B. Jordan, and all women would have a body like Jennifer Lopez, and we'd all be rich! The good news is that there are several strategies you can implement to improve your ability to choose delayed gratification. Here are some of them (they worked for me, so I'm hoping they'll work for you):

- **Break Down Your Goals:** The thought of writing a 100,000-word book isn't very appealing; in fact, it sounds like an impossible task. But when you break that down to 1000 words a day over 100 days, it doesn't sound so bad after all. When you're faced with the choice of trying to write a 100,000-word book or watching your favorite program on Netflix, you're likely going to choose the easier option. However, there's more chance of you choosing to write 1000 words before watching your favorite program on Netflix.

- **Commit in Advance:** One of the best ways to protect yourself against instant gratification is by making a commitment to yourself in advance. You can solidify that commitment by preparing for it. For example, if you've set yourself a weight-loss goal that involves going for a 30-minute run every morning, put your running shoes by your bedroom door and hang your running clothes in a place where you can see them as soon as you wake up.

- **Consider Your Future Feelings:** Think about how your future self will feel if you choose to sit in front of the TV instead of working on your goals. I used to imagine that my future self was watching me from another dimension. He was dying to switch places with me, and every time I made a bad choice, I delayed giving him the life he was so desperate to live. I found this strategy very helpful because it made me realize that the bad choices I was making were hindering my own progress.

THE INSTANT GRATIFICATION MONKEY

I took this idea from Tim Urban's blog. I found his concepts really insightful, and I'm sure you will too. Basically, Tim invented an instant gratification monkey who lives in the brain of chronic procrastinators. It's always fighting with the more intelligent lodger in the brain—the rational decisionmaker. But the monkey always wins. The problem with the monkey winning is that once it's hijacked the brain, it makes the worst decisions. The instant gratification monkey doesn't believe in delayed gratification; it doesn't understand the rational decisionmaker because its whole purpose is to live an easy life. It will tell you to stop jogging because taking a break on that bench will feel much better. It tells you to stop practicing for that singing competition because scrolling through social media is a lot more fun. It tells you to eat that donut because it tastes better than a salad. I think you get my point.

The monkey is the loudest voice in the head of a procrastinator, but it doesn't win all the time, because it has an enemy. That enemy is the panic monster, who turns up when a deadline is around the corner and the only way to avoid failure is to go to extremes like staying up all night to complete the project to rectify the situation. Most instant gratification monkeys do a runner when the panic monster shows up, and the procrastinator can finally do what they need to do. On the surface, the panic monster sounds like a lifesaver, because at least you managed to finish the project. But over the long term, doing things at the last minute is not a good idea. Here's why:

- The procrastinator will eventually fail to meet their goals. They will become an underachiever and never reach their full potential. This results in regret, guilt, and self-esteem issues.

- The procrastinator will always get the urgent projects done, but they will never do the things they want to do. In other words, anything that doesn't have a strict deadline that activates the panic monster will never get done.

GET INTO A ROUTINE TO STOP WASTING TIME

Not knowing where to start was always a problem for me, and one of the main reasons why I procrastinated so much. I would always sit around twiddling my thumbs for hours on end because I was overwhelmed. But that changed once I got myself into a solid routine. According to Isaac Newton's first law of motion, an object will stay still unless force is used to move it, and an object in motion will stay in motion. In other words, the key to developing good habits is to get started. The problem is that it takes a lot of energy to get moving, and you've got to be willing to make that initial investment. Let's use a rocket as an example. According to physics, the rocket will need more force than its weight to get it moving. To keep the rocket moving, the thrust needs to be equal to the weight and the air resistance, but it doesn't need as much power as the first thrust to keep it moving because it's now in motion. The same applies to your habits—it will get easier as you keep moving forward. Here are some tips on how to stop wasting time and start getting things done:

Make a To-Do List: Instead of trying to remember everything you've got to get done, write out a to-do list before you go to bed. Think about all your commitments for the following day and write them down. No matter how small the task, put it on paper. The next step is to arrange the list in order of priority by putting a number next to each item. If I've got a lot to do for that day, I find it very helpful to group items together; for example, phoning clients and responding to emails can be put into a "client communication" group.

Reduce Your Timeframe: Parkinson's law suggests that when people have less time to complete a project, they work on it faster than if they had more time to get it done. Block out less time for each task to trick your brain into thinking it needs to work faster.

Reward Yourself: Once you've completed everything on your to-do list, give yourself a reward. One of my guilty pleasures that wasted a lot of my time watching YouTube videos. I could scroll and watch for hours without a second thought. I would always tell myself, "One more video"—and before I knew it, it was time to go to bed. The brain is motivated by rewards; if it knows it's going to get something pleasurable, it will prompt you to plough through the task so you can get your reward. Once I had finished everything on my to-do list, I would reward myself by watching two YouTube videos. It was a powerful motivator for me.

Take Regular Breaks: I thought I was on the right track when I would work for three hours straight without taking a break. I really thought I was grinding and getting somewhere. But what I was really doing was slowing myself down. After those three hours, I was burned out, and the rest of my day was unproductive. But when I started taking regular breaks, I was very productive for a full eight hours. I would take a ten-minute break every hour, get up from my desk, stretch, walk around, or go and get a glass of water. During the summer months, I'd go for a quick walk outside. A break refreshed me and gave me clarity of mind because I knew I would free myself from the task in an hour.

Eliminate Distractions: Randomly checking emails and text messages or taking phone calls is a major distraction, especially if what you read or hear needs your urgent attention. I found that once I turned off all notifications and put my phone on "do not disturb," I was much more productive. I now only check my phone and emails twice a day: in the morning after I've completed my daily routine and I'm ready to start my day, and right at the end of the day, once all the tasks on my to-do lists are complete. Let me warn you—your friends and family members are going to get offended that you no longer respond to their messages immediately. Don't let that get to you though because you've got to do what's right for you. Also, you might be worried about only checking emails twice a day—what if you miss something important from work? I thought the same—but think about it like this: back in the day, when we didn't have Internet access on our phones, and not everyone had a computer at home, we could go a day or two without checking our emails—yet businesses still ran smoothly, and no one lost any sleep over it. So, I don't think it'll be too much of a problem if it takes you five hours to respond to someone's email.

Don't make the mistake of checking your phone during your ten-minute break. It might seem harmless, but you'll be surprised at how easy it is to extend your ten-minute break to an hour once you find something that gets your attention.

Tell People Not to Interrupt You: If you work from home, or you work on your long-term goals after work, let your partner and children know not to interrupt you. You can further enforce this by closing your door and putting a "do not disturb" sign on it. Interruptions from people are just as bad as distractions from your phone. So, don't shy away from telling your nearest and dearest to keep their distance when you're working.

Stick to Your Routine: Finally, do your best to stick to the routine and refuse to compromise. Don't do things like decide to check your emails more than normal or turn on your notifications. Once you start cutting corners, you'll get back into the habit of instant gratification, and before you know it, you'll have taken two steps backwards instead of forwards.

Establish a Good Bedtime Routine

According to the Centers for Disease Control, Americans don't get enough sleep. I was definitely in that statistic; my old bedtime routine was to fall asleep really late with my phone in my hand! Sometimes I'd muster up the strength to turn the light off and draw the curtains; sometimes I wouldn't. Even if I did get eight hours' sleep, I always woke up feeling groggy. A bedtime routine is just as important as a morning routine. Once I'd established one, I became even more productive during the day.

A bedtime routine involves engaging in a set of activities in the same order 30 to 60 minutes each night before going to sleep. What you choose to do during this time is up to you, but they are typically calming activities such as meditation, journaling, reading, or taking a warm bath. A bedtime routine is important because humans are creatures of habit, and our brains need a reminder that it's time to sleep. It also helps reduce nighttime stress and anxiety. In general, people do most of their worrying before they fall asleep, and an anxious mind prevents you from falling into a deep sleep and getting proper rest. Rumination and anxious thoughts activate the sympathetic nervous system and your mind. If these thoughts are left to fester without you taking control over them, you'll end up with insomnia. A bedtime routine will help the body relax and guard the mind against worrisome thoughts. Here are some tips on how to establish a good bedtime routine:

Utilize Your Sleep-Wake Cycle: The brain starts shutting down a few hours before bedtime as a part of the body's natural sleep-wake cycle. A bedtime routine will make this process more effective. Decide what time you're going to go to bed and wake up every day—and stick to it. A consistent sleep routine will train your brain to feel tired when it's time to sleep. After a while, you will notice that you naturally wake up and go to sleep at these times because your brain will have become trained to do so. The next step is to choose a time to start your nighttime routine. It can be anywhere between 30 minutes to two hours before you go to sleep. Remind yourself with an alarm clock if you know you might forget.

No Mobile Devices: This one was another game-changer for me. I used to literally fall asleep with the phone to my ear. We've been duped into thinking that scrolling or watching TV can help you relax. Just think of all those cozy-looking adverts showing people lounging on the sofa watching a movie. However, what they don't tell you is that electronic devices such as your smartphone, tablet, and television emit strong blue light that tricks the brain into thinking it's daytime. Your brain then starts slowing down the production of melatonin (the chemical that helps you sleep) so you can stay awake. To stop playing tricks on your brain, stop looking at electronic devices at night. If you are typically glued to your phone, and you know you'll find this difficult, turn on its red-light filter a few hours before starting your bedtime routine so that if you pick up your phone by accident, it won't affect you as much.

Have Something to Eat: Going to sleep on an empty stomach can be just as disruptive as going to sleep full. Eating a heavy meal can cause acid reflux, indigestion, and have you getting up in the middle of the night to use the toilet. But going to bed on an empty stomach can make it harder for you to fall asleep because your brain is focusing on the hunger signals your stomach is sending it. When you do finally get to sleep, you won't fall into a deep sleep because your brain is working overtime because of your hunger pains. Avoid this by having a light snack such as oats, nuts, strawberries, grapes, or cherries. It's also important to mention that these foods have a high melatonin content, which will help you fall asleep. Non-caffeinated herbal teas such as lavender or chamomile calm the mind and promote sleep.

Soak in the Bathtub: The body goes through several hormonal changes throughout the day as part of the sleep-wake cycle. One of the hormones released during the night is melatonin. As melatonin is released, your core body temperature also drops. According to scientists, you can replicate that drop in body temperature by having a warm bath. The water will warm you up, and as it evaporates, it will cool you down. The warming up and cooling down effect makes you feel relaxed and tired.

Play Some Tunes: Studies have found that 62 percent of people listen to music to help them get to sleep. It doesn't matter what type of music you listen to as long as it relaxes you. Audio such as pink or white noise and ambient sounds will also help you fall asleep. Research suggests that white noise helps you sleep faster, and pink noise improves sleep quality.

Relaxation Techniques: Progressive muscle relaxation (PMR), and breathing exercises help to induce sleep because they assist in the release of mental and physical tension. Studies have also found that practicing yoga every day improves sleep quality. If you are prone to cramps during the night, a massage or simple stretching can help prevent them. Give each of these a try, see what works best for you, and incorporate it into your nighttime routine.

Clear Your Mind with Meditation: Meditation has the same effect as yoga in terms of improving sleep quality. One of the aims of mindfulness meditation is to train people to manage their thoughts and emotions so they don't spend the night stressed out and worried about the issues they are dealing with. There are plenty of guided meditations available online.

Read a Book: Most parents read to their children before bedtime; I definitely remember my parents doing it. We typically discontinue this habit once we grow out of it. But it's a great way to fall asleep; I prefer to read educational non-fiction books because genres like action and suspense defeat the purpose of having a nighttime routine and have you up all night to finish reading them.

Write in Your Journal/To-Do List: According to research, journaling has a restorative effect. By doing it in the evening, you get to manage your thoughts and emotions before sleeping. If journaling isn't your thing, write out a to-do list for the next day. Writing out a to-do list will also help you get to sleep because you will be clear on what you need to do instead of trying to work it out in your mind when you should be asleep.

Get Your Bedroom Ready: Making your bedroom sleep-ready will also benefit you. Make your room dark, quiet, and cool; change the temperature to 60-71 degrees Fahrenheit. Turn off any electronics with background noise. Pull down your blackout curtains and dim the lights. Remove any clutter, and use an aromatherapy diffuser with your favorite fragrance if you wish. The final step is to go to bed; make sure you've done everything that you need to do that day, so that you don't keep getting in and out of bed.

We've covered a lot so far, and I'm hoping you've already started to implement the strategies mentioned. But there are still a few more things I'd like to teach you that will further assist you in becoming all that you know you were destined to become. In the next chapter, you'll learn about how food can hinder your progress, and how to ditch bad eating habits and start consuming the foods that will supercharge your body and empower you to succeed.

CHAPTER 9:

EAT YOUR WAY TO SUCCESS

love food, and once upon a time, I had a terrible diet that consisted of fast food and sodas. I was shocked to find out how much food can influence your ability to succeed in life. Maintaining concentration and focus throughout the day is essential to your productivity. It is true that there are a lot of ways you can improve your concentration through being more mindful, taking short naps, developing your own focus formula, etc. But food has a major impact on how we feel throughout the day. The brain is a tiny little organ, but it's extremely powerful. I have come to the conclusion that it's more dangerous than a nuclear weapon! Think about it for a minute…There would be no nuclear weapons if it weren't for the human brain. It was thought about before it was created. Anyway, that's an entirely different issue. But you'll be amazed to know that the brain is so small it only accounts for two percent of your weight; however, it uses 20 percent of the energy produced by the body. If you don't provide the right nutrients for your brain, after a while you'll start experiencing symptoms such as fatigue, memory loss, and concentration problems.

If you're trying to break bad habits and replace them with good ones, you can't afford to have low energy. I know from personal experience that when you can't be bothered to do something, you choose the easiest option. I would rather talk on the phone than engage my brain in my financial management course. Or I'd rather watch TV instead of get my house in order. As you will soon read, there is plenty of research suggesting that healthy foods fuel your brain in the right way, allowing you to operate to your highest potential. In general, the most successful people in the world consume an extremely healthy diet. Now, I know this isn't true for all successful people, but it really does help. Would you like to know what some of your heroes eat during the day? Keep reading to find out...

Andy Murray: The former world number one tennis player eats salmon and rice for lunch and has plenty of protein shakes when he's training.

Nicole Scherzinger: The former Pussycat Doll eats plenty of blueberries and pineapples, and often has a large portion of vegetables with three slices of turkey for lunch.

Gwyneth Paltrow: The successful Hollywood actress promotes healthy living and wellness on her lifestyle website. She told *Vogue* magazine that she usually has grilled chicken and a large salad for lunch.

Novak Djokovic: The tennis star enjoys plenty of vegetables and some form of carbohydrate for lunch. He doesn't eat any foods containing gluten, and stays away from caffeine, dairy, and refined sugar.

Madonna: The singer's diet is slightly extreme, and you probably won't find a lot of what she eats in a regular supermarket.

Her diet consists of sea vegetables wakame, kelp, and nori. She stays away from meat, eggs, dairy and wheat.

Michelle Obama: The former first lady enjoys stir-fried vegetables and fish with potatoes or brown rice for lunch. She also has a love for vegetable pizzas on whole-wheat bread.

Obviously, a healthy diet isn't the only reason these people are successful, but it's definitely a very important piece of the puzzle.

FOODS THAT MAKE YOU FEEL LAZY AND TIRED

What typically happens after you've finished eating an entire large pizza and washed it down with a liter of Coke? You just want to veg out in front of the TV or go to sleep—right? Well, that's because it's been scientifically proven that eating junk food makes you lazy. Research conducted by UCLA found that eating high-fat, processed, and sugary foods leads to decreased performance, a lack of motivation, and tiredness. The study involved putting two groups of female rats on a healthy and an unhealthy diet. The healthy rat diet consisted of unprocessed foods such as fish meal and ground corn. The unhealthy rat diet consisted of highly processed, high-sugar foods similar to the junk foods that humans eat. After three months, the rats on the unhealthy diet not only put on weight, they also got lazy.

The rats had to perform a task that involved pressing a lever to receive a reward of food or water. The rats on the junk-food diet found this difficult and would take longer breaks than the rats on the healthy diet.

Here are some of the foods you will need to avoid if you're going to have enough motivation to break bad habits:

Granola and Energy Bars: I know, I know—I thought the same thing when I found out. These snacks are advertised as healthy, but they're not. They're loaded with fats, sugars, and carbohydrates, all of which are full of additives that can destabilize blood-sugar levels.

Condiments: As much as they make your fries and burgers taste good, condiments are terribly unhealthy. They are extremely high in additives and sugar; they're also high in sodium, which can make you feel dehydrated, lethargic and bloated. Condiments are one of the many reasons you want to fall asleep after lunch.

Pasta: The "carb coma" really is a thing; after eating a large bowl of spaghetti bolognaise—not to mention the garlic bread—for lunch, the last thing you're going to want to do is go to the gym after work. While it is better to eat whole-wheat pasta, it's still not ideal if you need to get stuff done. If you really feel like pasta, eat it on a day that you've got nothing to do, or have a small portion.

Dark Chocolate: Dark chocolate is super healthy—it's packed with anti-inflammatory and anti-aging antioxidants; it helps fight depression because of its serotonin content, and it's also good for the heart. The problem is that it contains a bit of caffeine, which will give you a quick energy boost, but you'll crash shortly after. Additionally, serotonin makes you sleepy, so it's a good treat to have in the evening as it will help you wind down before bedtime.

Sweet Snacks: Most snacks contain artificial sweeteners; not only do they make you feel sluggish, tired, and bloated, but research has found that they can also cause memory impairment, cancer, and weight gain.

Hamburgers: While lean protein is a good source of energy, hamburgers are typically cooked in grease which is high in unhealthy fats. My first job was in McDonald's, and I remember how they used to dump the fries and burgers in grease. I didn't think anything of it at the time—all I cared about was that the food tasted good, and that I could eat as many burgers as I liked. I don't eat hamburgers anymore, from McDonald's or any other fast-food restaurant, because research has found that they increase your risk of coronary heart disease, and type-2 diabetes.

FOODS THAT GIVE YOU ENERGY AND IMPROVE YOUR FOCUS

Essentially, all foods give you energy, even the foods that are bad for you. Food is fuel for the body; when you're hungry, you start feeling weak. Eating a bag of chips will give you some energy, even though you'll crash shortly after. But most healthy foods (and I say *most* because some of them can make you feel tired) provide you with a continuous source of energy to get you through the day. Here are some foods that give you energy and improve your focus:

Fatty Fish: Fatty fish such as tuna and salmon are good sources of B vitamins, protein, and fatty acids. One serving of either will provide you with the recommended daily amount of vitamin B12 and Omega-3 fatty acids. Omega-3 fatty acids help reduce inflammation, which is a common cause of fatigue. Also, the combination of vitamin B12 and folate assists in the production of

DANIEL WALTER

red blood cells, which increase the effects of iron. Iron and optimal levels of red blood cells increase energy and reduce fatigue.

Bananas: You will always see athletes eating bananas because they're a powerful source of vitamin B6, potassium, and complex carbs—all of which provide a significant boost in energy levels.

Sweet Potatoes: I love sweet potatoes—they are so delicious! They are a good source of complex carbohydrates and fiber, which are slowly digested, providing a steady supply of energy.

Green Tea: This popular warm beverage is made up of several components that improve brain health. It is rich in antioxidants and polyphenols, which protect the brain against mental decline and reduce the risk of Parkinson's and Alzheimer's disease. Studies have also found that it improves memory.

Brown Rice: I always hated brown rice; I found it too hard and tasteless. But there are ways you can cook it that will have you hooked. Since this isn't a cookbook, you can find some great ideas on YouTube. There are two grams of fiber in half a cup of brown rice. It also contains manganese, a mineral used by enzymes to turn carbohydrates and protein into energy. Also, brown rice has a low glycemic index because of its fiber content, which helps regulate blood-sugar levels so you have a steady source of energy throughout the day.

Blueberries: Blueberries provide several health benefits, one of which is powering the brain. They contain plant pigments called anthocyanins, which have antioxidant and anti-inflammatory effects. The antioxidants protect the brain against aging and neurodegenerative diseases. Studies have also found that they boost communication between brain cells. A review of 11 separate studies discovered that blueberries improve certain cognitive processes and memory. You can add them to a smoothie or sprinkle them over your breakfast cereal.

Eggs: Eggs are a high-protein food. They also contain the amino acid leucine, which stimulates energy production in a number of ways. Additionally, eggs are rich in vitamin B, which helps enzymes turn food into energy.

Broccoli: Broccoli is high in vitamin K. Research has found that vitamin K is linked to improved cognitive status and memory.

Goji Berries: These high-fiber berries slow down the digestion process so that energy is slowly released into the body.

Quinoa: This grain is a rich source of dietary fiber, carbohydrates, and protein. It has a low glycemic index, so carbs are slowly released, providing a sustainable energy release. Also, quinoa is high in folate and manganese, both of which play an important role in providing energy for the body.

Turmeric: Turmeric is one of the main ingredients in curry powder; it contains curcumin. Studies have found that as soon as it's consumed, it enters the brain and strengthens the cells. It also helps them grow. Curcumin has been found to improve memory in people suffering from Alzheimer's disease.

Natural Yogurt: Flavored yogurt is one of the many snacks that is advertised as a health-food product, when in actual fact it is laced with sugar. But natural yogurt contains simple sugars such as galactose and lactose, which provide a steady supply of energy. Natural yogurt also contains plenty of protein.

Hummus: Made from tahini, olive oil, lemon, and chickpeas, hummus is a powerful source of energy. Chickpeas contain fiber and complex carbs, which the body uses for energy; tahini and olive oil are healthy fats, which slow down carbohydrate absorption, protecting the body against blood-sugar spikes.

Lentils: Lentils are high in fiber and carbohydrates; they increase energy levels by refueling the body with iron, zinc, and manganese. These nutrients give the cells energy so that they are better able to break down the nutrients required for energy release.

Pumpkin Seeds: They are a powerful source of copper, zinc, iron, and magnesium, all of which are good for the brain. Zinc is required for nerve signaling; magnesium for memory and learning. Copper is required to control nerve signals, and iron improves brain fog.

Avocados: This superfood contains fiber, B vitamins, and healthy fats, which boost the body's ability to absorb nutrients. Healthy fats are also stored in the body and used as an energy reserve.

Oranges: Most people know that oranges are good for vitamin C, but they also contain antioxidant compounds that protect the body against oxidative stress. Studies have found that oxidative stress leads to tiredness.

Nuts: There are several nutrients in nuts, including vitamin E, antioxidants, and healthy fats that help to improve brain function.

Research has found that regular consumption of nuts keeps the brain healthy. Individuals who eat them have a sharper memory in comparison to those who don't.

EAT WHEN YOU WAKE UP

As mentioned, I never had breakfast at home because I was always running late. I'd then get something unhealthy on my way to work. By mid-morning I was starving again and would resort to crisps, cereal bars, or chocolate to keep me going until lunchtime. Wake up a bit earlier and have a healthy breakfast; the reason why eating when you wake up is called "break-fast" is because you are literally breaking a six- to eight-hour fast, depending on how much sleep you've had. During the night, your metabolism slows down, and if you run out the door without getting any fuel in your tank, you'll feel sluggish. A healthy breakfast could include whole-grain toast with cheese, nut butter, or boiled or poached eggs. Or natural yogurt filled with live probiotics, and honey. You can also have some fruits such as an orange or a banana to start your day off with some essential nutrients. Wholefoods are beneficial because they are better for your digestive system, and they take longer to digest, which means you'll stay full until lunchtime.

Have a Healthy Lunch: Whether you work from home or at an office, it's good to get out of your environment at lunchtime. Clear your head, stretch your legs, and eat something nutritious and healthy. As delicious as they are, avoid sandwiches smothered in mayonnaise, pizza, burgers, sweets, and cakes. Instead, opt for a delicious salad made with a variety of ingredients such as sprouting grains, mixed leaves, spring onions, radishes, peppers, beetroot, artichokes, kidney beans, and chickpeas.

Your Fluid Intake: Sodas and fruit juices are tasty but ridiculously unhealthy. It's advised that you drink water throughout the day. This makes sense, considering the body is made up of 60 percent water. It's argued that adults should drink at least eight eight-ounce glasses of water per day, but there isn't much scientific data to back this up. Either way, hydration is important for several reasons. Here are some of them:

- **It Affects Brain Function and Energy Levels:** I drink two liters of water a day, and I noticed a massive difference when I started doing this. I used to be an avid energy drink and coffee drinker, and the dip after the high was always terrible. I would either have to drink some more or take a nap; the nap was always disastrous—I would set my alarm clock for 20 minutes and wake up three hours later. If it was during the day, I'd immediately reach for another energy drink or cup of coffee so I could get on with what I needed to do. If it was in the evening, I'd just go right back to sleep. Basically, I was sleeping my life away—but that all changed when I started drinking water.

  The brain is made up of 85 percent water. It depends on water for the required electrical energy. The brain uses twice as much water as all the other cells in the body. It's also important to mention that, out of all other substances, water is the most efficient energy source. Neurotransmitters such as norepinephrine and dopamine, which are responsible for improved executive functioning, and other hormones in the brain also depend on water. Studies have found that when you give your body the right amount of water, your thinking speed increases by 14 percent, you become more creative, and you can focus for longer. Research has also shown that even mild dehydration can have a negative effect on brain function. In one study, it was found that fluid loss after exercise made it difficult for participants to concentrate and put them in a bad mood.

• **Treats and Prevents Headaches:** Headaches, be gone! I always had headaches, and I was constantly taking painkillers to relieve them. What I didn't know was that I was severely dehydrated, and headaches are one of the most common symptoms of this. Studies have found that drinking water can help to relieve the tension associated with headaches.

• **Helps Prevent Hangovers:** Now, one of the habits I haven't given up is drinking! I've toned it down a bit, but I still go out every once in a while and have a few drinks. Have you ever noticed that you're always running to the toilet when you have a drink? That's because alcohol is a diuretic, and it makes you lose fluids, which causes dehydration. Some of the symptoms of dehydration are headaches, dry mouth, and fatigue, all of which contribute to a terrible hangover. You can limit the effects of a hangover by drinking one glass of water between every glass of alcohol, and one large glass of water before you go to bed.

• **Helps with Weight Loss:** Water boosts your metabolic rate and increases satiety, which means you won't feel as hungry. Some studies have found that water assists with the weight-loss process because it speeds up the metabolism, and this increases the number of calories you burn each day. A study conducted in 2013 found that overweight women who drank an extra 500 ml of water three times a day before dinner for eight weeks experienced a noticeable reduction in body fat and body weight in comparison to their measurements before the study.

- **Helps Treat Kidney Stones:** If you're suffering from kidney stones, drinking plenty of water might help them pass through your system. Drinking more water means that more urine travels through the kidneys. This dilutes the mineral concentration, making the stones less likely to crystalize and form clumps. There is also some evidence that drinking enough water prevents them from forming in the first place.

You can have your tea and coffee—just don't drink too much, because caffeine dehydrates the body and makes you anxious. Also, stay away from energy drinks; they might boost your energy levels temporarily, but you'll crash shortly after and need another one, hence the vicious cycle that comes with consuming such drinks. The bottom line is, stay away from drinks loaded with artificial sweeteners.

HOW TO DRINK MORE WATER THROUGHOUT THE DAY

Like me, you might find it difficult to drink water, and prefer sodas or juices. But as you're probably aware of by now, that's not what you need—so here are a few tips on how you can drink more water.

Set a Goal: Science has proven that the brain likes goals. But the brain doesn't like big goals, and it will shut down on you and revert to its comfort zone when you try to set them. So, instead of trying to convince yourself to drink two liters of water a day, break it down. For example, you can start by making sure you have one glass of water with each meal. "Well, that's only three glasses," I hear you saying. Yes, I know—the aim is to get started.

Track Your Progress: Habits are easier to develop when you can see the progress you're making. I added water drinking to my daily to-do list—I simply entered: "Drink 3 glasses of water: 1, 2, 3." I carried that notebook with me everywhere I went, and when I drank a glass of water, I would cross it off. I found this very satisfying! You can also use a "drink water" app reminder if you prefer.

Bring a Bottle: If you're on the go, buy a water bottle, fill it up before you leave the house, and carry it with you. I would always forget to drink water when I left the house, so carrying a bottle was the most efficient way to get my daily intake.

Habit-Linking: Habit-linking involves linking your habits with other habits you're developing; for example:

- Have a glass of water before and after the gym.
- Have a glass of water when you wake up and before you go to bed
- Have a glass of water before and after you study.

TIPS FOR EATING A HEALTHY DIET

Eating a healthy diet sounds good in theory, but in practice it can be just as difficult to kick eating junk food as every other bad habit you've got. Therefore, you've got to make a conscious and determined effort to do so. Your first task is to educate yourself on what to eat, because if you don't know, how can you eat it—right? Here is a bit more insight into the foods you should be eating:

The healthy diet food pyramid helps you visualize what a healthy diet should look like and the types of foods you should be eating every day. The pyramid is made up of six layers:

Oils, Whole-Grain Foods: You should have these foods with every meal because they provide complex sugars and fiber, and the oils contain healthy fats. Examples of oils and whole grains include:

- Oatmeal
- Millet
- Bulgur
- Buckwheat
- Brown rice
- Whole-wheat bread, crackers, or pasta
- Canola oil
- Olive oil
- Avocado oil
- Walnut oil
- Flaxseed oil

Fruits and Vegetables: Experts recommend having at least 2-3 servings of fruits and vegetables per day. Examples of fruits and vegetables include:

- Bananas
- Ginger
- Garlic
- Bell peppers
- Leafy green vegetables
- Tomatoes
- Apples
- Strawberries

Eggs, Poultry, and Fish: These foods are a great source of protein. You should add at least two portions a day to your meals.

- Chicken
- Turkey
- Salmon
- Mackerel

Dairy Products: You don't need to consume many dairy products throughout the week. Although they contain vital minerals and nutrients such as calcium, they are also high in fat and protein. Examples of dairy products include:

- Milk
- Cheese
- Cream cheese
- Yogurt
- Butter

Sticking to a healthy diet is difficult. In Chapter 10, I will talk about the things you need to do to ensure you maintain your good habits. If you don't have certain things in place, you'll quickly fall back into eating junk food—which is what happened to me several times before I started applying the strategies I'm going to mention now.

Learn to Cook: Today you have no excuse if you don't know how to cook because the Internet is awash with recipes and "how to" videos giving you step-by-step instructions on how to make a variety of dishes. The easiest way to eat a healthy diet is to cook your own food, because you know what you're putting in it. Plus, there's so much more to choose from. Have you noticed that a junk-food diet typically consists of pizza, burgers, and fries? Gets a bit boring after a while, don't you think?

Go Shopping Weekly: One of the things that contributed to me eating an unhealthy diet was that I never had any food in the house. My cupboards were perpetually empty, and the contents of my fridge consisted of moldy pizza and spoiled milk. But things changed once I started going shopping weekly and making sure I had everything I needed to make my meals in the house.

Don't Go Shopping on an Empty Stomach: When you're hungry, you're more likely to snack. I used to go to the store with good intentions, but because my stomach was growling, I'd either buy something unhealthy to snack on, or pass through a drive-through and get a burger. Even though I'd still go to the store and buy my healthy stuff, I kept rekindling my appetite for unhealthy foods. Once I realized it was because I kept going to the store on an empty stomach, I'd go after lunch instead. It's amazing how much of a difference it made.

Avoid Unhealthy Food Aisles: The unhealthy foods are all located in the same place. The sweets, cakes, candy, and chocolate have their own aisle. Instead of walking down these aisles and tempting yourself, avoid them altogether. Go straight to the healthy food sections and bypass the rest.

As mentioned, replacing bad habits with good ones isn't an easy process. You've been eating junk food, procrastinating, and watching too much TV for years, so you're not going to snap out of it tomorrow. But with some dedication and perseverance, you can replace your bad habits with good ones. Keep reading to find out how.

CHAPTER 10:

THE SECRET TO REPLACING YOUR BAD HABITS

I f you've got to this chapter, I can only assume you've reached that stage in your life where you're sick and tired of being sick and tired, and you're ready to make a change. I'm hoping that by now you understand that you're not going to become the best version of yourself overnight, and it's going to take some work. But it's also important to understand that getting started will be the most difficult part of your journey.

GETTING STARTED IS THE HARDEST PART

Getting started on this journey of developing good habits is the most difficult obstacle to overcome. My favorite words during that time were, "I'll start tomorrow." Six months down the line, and I had yet to see tomorrow. Other than pure laziness, there are many reasons why starting is the hardest part when it comes to making changes in your life. One of my biggest fears was the fear of success. I know, it sounds strange, doesn't it? How can you be afraid of living the life of your dreams? Let's take a look at some of the reasons why getting started is so hard.

The Fear of Success: What happens when you overcome all your bad habits and become super successful? Your life will change drastically—and I just wasn't ready for it. It all goes back to staying in your comfort zone. You know what your life is like; you're used to living this way—and now you've got to step into another dimension that you know nothing about. Subconsciously, I wanted to remain in a place where I was familiar with everything. Or maybe you're afraid of what your friends and family members will think once you start working on that project. What happens if someone at your sophisticated job finds out your side hustle is a bit on the unserious side? What if you do become a *New York Times* bestselling author—how are you going to keep up such a high standard? For me, the fear of success had the same power as the fear of failure; they were both preventing me from moving forward.

You Don't Have the Support: When I told my parents I was quitting my job as an investment banker to become an author, they were not impressed. As far as they were concerned, an author wasn't a proper job, and they hadn't invested all that money into my private school education for me to become a starving writer. I had zero support—none from my friends or my family. They thought what I was doing was completely and utterly ridiculous. When you value the opinion of your friends and family members, and you care what other people think about you, the last thing you want to do is end up in a situation where they don't agree with what you're doing. But you can't live like this, or you'll never get anywhere in life. If following your dreams means you need to cut some people off or keep them at arm's length, then that's what you've got to do.

You Feel Lost: I have a friend who has a very successful clothing line, but it took him several years to get it off the ground because he didn't know where to start. He was a gifted designer, and he knew exactly how he wanted his clothes to look. But there were so many things he didn't understand, so he just buried his head in the sand. His story is extremely inspiring. He remembers how his friends used to mock him because he was always showing them his designs but no one ever saw the finished product. They referred to him as "the dreamer." As far as they were concerned, he was never going to make it.

Your Priorities Are Wrong: When I enrolled in my financial management course, why did I think it was more important to spend hours talking to my friends on the phone trying to resolve their issues than focusing on my own personal development? I wasted so much time on menial tasks that I didn't have time to do what was really important. I later learned that my time-wasting endeavors were all connected to my fear of getting started. I was basically using everything else I was doing as an excuse not to work on what I knew would help me succeed.

A Lack of Confidence: You might be ready to get started working on your dreams, but you don't have the confidence to follow it through. You've got everything planned out, but deep down you don't feel as if you're good enough to pull it off. This is especially true if you're a perfectionist and hate the thought of failure; you will remain stagnant because you don't think you're good enough to get it right.

So, when it comes to replacing your bad habits with good ones, getting started is the hardest part—but it's more than possible; I've done it and so have many others. If you want to find out how, keep reading.

HOW TO REPLACE YOUR BAD HABITS

The secret to replacing your bad habits is in your motivation. If you're doing it because your friend, spouse, brother, or sister is doing it, you'll quit before you get started. But if you know deep within that you want to change your bad habits, you've started building the foundation you need to succeed. You see, in the same way you can't build a building without a solid foundation, you can't change your bad habits without a strong foundation. That foundation is desire, and once you've got it, you can start building. The first stage of the building process is to reprogram your subconscious mind.

REPROGRAM YOUR SUBCONSCIOUS MIND

In Chapter 1, I spoke about the power of the subconscious mind and how it keeps you chained to your bad habits. In this chapter, I will discuss how you can reprogram your subconscious mind for success.

Self-Suggestion: Before you go to sleep, direct your subconscious mind towards your desired results by using self-suggestion. This involves writing out a statement that describes the new habits you want to develop. Read the statement out loud several times before you sleep and when you wake up in the morning.

Abundance and Success Statement: This is similar to self-suggestion, but it involves writing out a statement for abundance and success. You want to develop good habits for a reason—what is that reason? Read this statement several times before you go to sleep and when you wake up in the morning.

Positive Affirmations: Repeating affirmations by writing them out, saying them, or listening to them while you sleep is one of the fastest ways to reprogram your subconscious mind. When developing your affirmations, write them in the present tense as if you already have them. Avoid using words such as, "I need," or, "I want"—instead use words such as, "I am," or, "I have." Your subconscious mind can't tell the difference between what's real and what's not. Using words that suggest you already have what you want will raise your vibrational frequency, and you'll start attracting your desired results. Your job is to pay attention to the opportunities when they arrive and take them.

Record Your Affirmations: The subconscious mind is most familiar with your own voice because that's what it hears every day. Therefore, you can influence your mind faster when you record your own affirmations and play them on repeat while you sleep.

No Devices Before Bedtime: Turn off all your electrical devices at least 90 minutes before you go to bed. The purpose of this is to slow down brain activity and your subconscious mind. As mentioned, the blue light emitted from devices such as computers, tablets, laptops, and cell phones hinders and interrupts the release of the sleep hormone melatonin. As a result, it prevents you from falling into a deep sleep—and a good night's sleep is necessary if you are going to effectively reprogram your subconscious mind. To remove the temptation of glancing at your phone or other gadgets when you're in bed, turn them off and put them in another room. A lot of people use their phone as an alarm clock. This is a bad idea—buy a cheap alarm clock from Amazon instead.

Meditation: There are several benefits associated with meditation, and one of them is that it slows down the mind. When the mind is at rest, it gives you the ability to focus on your body and mind, which strengthens and energizes you. It also helps you release anxiety and stress. I was never into meditation because I assumed it was about emptying your mind and thinking about nothing. I tried this and found it impossible. Meditation is about training your mind to focus on one thought. It is the gateway to the subconscious mind and strengthens your connection to it. Here is the meditation I started out with—it only takes five minutes, and it's extremely effective:

- Set an alarm for five minutes.

- Sit in a comfortable and relaxed position on the floor on a cushion, or on a chair.

- Keep your back straight, but don't make it too stiff.

- Keep your hands in any position you feel comfortable.

- Pay attention to your body and relax; notice how heavy you feel, and your posture.

- As you relax, allow yourself to become curious about your body.

- Tune in to the sensations—your connection with the chair or the floor, how you feel.

- If you sense any areas of tension or tightness, relax these areas.

- Pay attention to your breath and feel its natural flow as you breathe in and out.

- Pay attention to where you feel your breath in your body.

- Pay attention to the sensations as you breathe.

- You will notice that your mind starts to wander. That's fine—just bring your attention back to your breath.

- Remain like this for five minutes until your alarm goes off.

Binaural Beats: Slowing down your thought waves will slow down the subconscious mind. You can achieve this using specific brainwave frequencies such as:

- *Delta (0Hz-4Hz):* Your brain goes into this frequency when you enter a deep sleep. The conscious mind is able to switch off completely, and the subconscious mind can take over and come up with plans for you to achieve your desired results.

- *Theta (4Hz-8Hz):* The theta frequency gets the brain into a trancelike or drowsy state. At this stage, the conscious mind is no longer responding to your thoughts. Using positive affirmations while listening to these binaural beats will boost results.

- *Alpha (8Hz-12Hz):* When it's time to slow down your thinking, alpha frequencies help shut the brain down so the body can relax.

- *Beta (12Hz-30Hz):* The beta frequency gets the mind into focus mode. Listening to these binaural beats will help you when you need to finish an important project and concentrate for long periods of time.

- *Gamma (30 Hz):* Helps your mind connect with the frequencies required for focus and thinking. If you've got a problem to solve, listen to some gamma binaural beats, and you will tap into your creative mind.

You can find binaural beats on YouTube, Spotify, Amazon Music, an app, or any other website where music is available.

Thought Dumping: You don't want to go to bed in a worried or anxious state with the day's events on your mind. You won't get a good night's sleep when your mind is weighed down with stress and anxiety. You can get rid of these negative thoughts by taking a few minutes to write out everything that's bothering you before you go to sleep. You can also write out a statement to help remove those thoughts from your mind. In this way, you are giving the subconscious mind the opportunity to forget about your worries and concentrate on solutions.

Listen to Music: Not all music provides the same value, but certain music without lyrics calms the mind. For example, nature sounds such as rain, wind, and the sound of the sea provide the same benefits as meditation. The vibrational frequency from classical music relaxes you and slows down your mental activity.

Nighttime Planning: Planning your day before you go to sleep allows your subconscious mind to work out how it's going to get everything done. While you sleep, it will organize your day so you are ready for action as soon as you wake up.

Use Auto-Suggestions: Auto-suggestions are triggers used to impress onto the subconscious mind. Place them in locations where you know you will see them several times a day. Examples of where to place them include:

- Vision board
- Cup or water bottle
- Desktop computer wallpaper
- Cell phone
- Mirror
- Post-it notes
- Goal cards.

Auto-suggestions can include:

1. A word such as:
   - Love
   - Happiness
   - Money
   - Abundance
   - Success

2. A weight-loss target or an exact amount of money:
   - Lose 20 lbs
   - Triple my yearly income
   - 10 million dollars

3. A statement:
   - I have met my soulmate by summer.
   - 1 have lost 20 lbs in weight within 6 months.
   - I have 10 million dollars in the bank by the age of 40.
   - I have tripled my yearly income within three years.

The more your subconscious mind is exposed to these auto-suggestions, the faster it is reprogrammed. Once your subconscious mind has been reprogrammed, the universe will start sending your desires to you. Your job is to take action when these opportunities and ideas present themselves to you.

USE THE THREE R'S TO BREAK BAD HABITS

According to management consultant Margaret Moore, you can break bad habits using the three R's:

- **Reminders:** You need something to remind you of your new habit

- **Routine:** The action you need to take to develop the new habit

- **Reward:** The benefit you will get out of changing your behavior

The three R's are all linked in a continuous loop. This is how it works: Let's say you have a bad habit of scrolling through social media when you have a project to complete. The loop is, after dinner (reminder), you sit at your desk, set up your laptop, and organize everything you need in order to start working on your project (routine). It's a difficult task, you're tired, and you don't want to do it. You say to yourself, "I'll just check Instagram for five minutes"—reward—"before getting started." But you end up scrolling for 30 minutes. You then decide to check YouTube and end up on there for another 30 minutes. By the time you're done, your brain and body have gone into complete relaxation mode, so you shut your laptop and tell yourself you'll get on with it tomorrow. The pleasure you get from scrolling through social media then gives you the desire to repeat the action when you get the next reminder.

UNDERSTAND YOUR REMINDER AND ROUTINE

The easiest way to break the bad habit should be just to stop scrolling through social media when you know you've got work to do. But it's not as simple as that because the problem isn't social media—it's the habit you've developed. Your first step in overcoming the bad habit is to get a better understanding of the reminder and the routine. In this case, once you've finished your dinner, you sit at your desk and take out your phone instead of getting on with the task. Now get a pen and paper, ask yourself why you get your phone out, and write down the answers using short, descriptive words or phrases that describe how you feel before you start the routine. Perhaps it is boredom? Or the anticipation you experience knowing you're going to see a post that interests you? Or the satisfaction of knowing you're delaying the project you don't want to work on?

The next step is to know your triggers; research suggests that habit triggers generally fall into five categories: after an action, people, emotional state, time, and location. With the scrolling-through-social-media scenario, these categories might look like this:

- After an action: After dinner
- Other people: Annoying partner
- Emotional state: Tired
- Time: 7:00 p.m.
- Location: Bedroom

Spend seven days paying attention to your behavior and, using the above categories, make notes. After one week, read back over what you've recorded and see if there are any patterns. For example, you might find it more difficult to get off social media after you've had an argument with your partner, or when you've finished work later than normal and you're feeling extra tired. When you can figure out what is contributing to your bad habits, you can change them.

Rewards: I briefly mentioned rewards in Chapter 8, but here I want to go into it in a little more detail. You can motivate yourself to stick to your good habits by rewarding yourself. Let me explain why the reward system is so powerful. Our thoughts and behaviors are shaped by neurotransmitters in the brain. The pleasure chemical, dopamine, is one of the main neurotransmitters in the brain's reward system. Dopamine is produced in the mid-brain before traveling to other parts of the brain such as the amygdala, which is the part of the brain responsible for our emotions. Dopamine is also transported to the prefrontal cortex, the part of the brain responsible for feeling, thinking, planning, and taking action.

When you do something you enjoy, the brain releases dopamine, which makes you feel good. This typically happens when we do something like have a stimulating conversation, have sex, or eat our favorite food. Anytime we experience pleasure, the memory of what made us feel good is stored in the subconscious mind, and the brain assigns it a reward value. So, eating your favorite hamburger will have a higher reward value than eating an apple. Or seeing your partner in person will have a higher reward value than looking at their photo. Just the mere thought of high-reward-value activities makes us happy because we get excited about the expectation of the reward, and it's the expectation that drives our behavior.

GOAL-SET YOUR WAY TO SUCCESS

I'm assuming that you want to break your bad habits because you want to be more successful in life. That was definitely the case for me; in addition to the health reasons, I knew that if I didn't change my habits, I would never accomplish the goals I kept setting for myself, but didn't achieve because they were so up in the air. At the beginning of every year, I'd say the same thing: "I'm going to write my book, stop smoking, lose weight, and save money." I didn't write these goals down, and I didn't formulate a plan to get me there. Goal-setting is important for many reasons. Here are some of them:

It Gives You Control Over Your Life: Until I started setting goals, I was sleepwalking through life. I was a very hard-working man, but I didn't feel as if I was getting anywhere. It was like walking on an uphill treadmill, moving but going nowhere. I didn't have a specific direction; I was moving, but I wasn't achieving anything. I was living on autopilot, and I wasn't living a life of my own conscious creation.

You Get the Best Results: All successful people, world-class athletes, and top performers set goals—Elon Musk, Richard Branson, Mark Zuckerberg, and Michael Phelps, to name a few. When you set goals, you have a vision to work towards, and you get the best results because you're pushing yourself in the direction of those goals instead of twiddling your thumbs and waiting for things to happen. You can improve what you measure. I weighed myself once a week to make sure I was on track—if I wasn't, I made improvements and upped my game to reach the targets I had set for myself. If you have no milestones and targets, you're literally throwing the arrows out there hoping they'll hit something—and that's not how life goes. Have you heard the saying, "Aim for the moon and even if you miss, you'll reach the stars"? In other words, you'll hit something as long as you've got an aim. To put it into context, even if I'd lost 50 pounds and not one hundred, I still would have lost something, and something is better than nothing.

They Give You Motivation: Goal-setting is the drive you need to get going. Think about it; what's there to be motivated about when you have nothing to look forward to? Let's say you set a goal to buy your first house within two years. Looking at your vision board and imagining how it will feel to be a homeowner are drivers to push you in the direction of achieving your goal.

Once I got focused on the outcome through planning, things started to change for me. Here are some tips on how to get stuff done and unleash the real you that's trapped inside your body just screaming to come out:

USE THE SMART GOAL METHOD

When I was introduced to the SMART goal method, I thought, "Does it really take all this?" The answer is yes! Success isn't an accident—you've got to plan for it. And the more meticulous you are about it, the more likely you are to succeed. So, what is the SMART goal method?

SMART is an acronym for goal-setting, and the specifics of how it works will depend on each individual, but in general, this is what you can expect:

- S: Specific
- M: Measurable
- A: Achievable
- R: Realistic
- T: Time-bound

"That's great, but what exactly does this mean?" A legitimate question—I thought the same when I first read it. Let me break this down to you a little further.

- **Specific:** As I've mentioned, vague goals will get you nowhere but walking around in circles until you're 40 years of age and you realize you haven't achieved anything. Unfortunately, that's the story of the majority of the world. If you want to start saving to buy a house, find out exactly how much you need so you have a specific amount to work towards. If you set a goal to get a higher-paying job, decide how much more money you want to earn, only apply for jobs that pay that much, and refuse to settle for anything less. If you are single and you want to get married, decide what characteristics you want in your partner, and hold off from dating until you find that person. Is this making sense?

- **Measurable:** Can you measure your goals? Back to the retirement plan: decide how much you want to save by retirement, and work out how much you need to put away each month to reach that goal.

- **Achievable:** I believe in the power of positive thinking—and yes, we can achieve anything we put our minds to. However, it's also easy to set yourself up for failure when you set goals that are impossible to achieve, for example, aiming to lose 100 pounds in two months! Even when you break it down, you are never going to achieve it. That's 50 pounds a month, and 12 pounds a week! Even if you're planning on starving yourself, you probably won't make it.

- **Realistic:** This is similar to "achievable." Let's say you've set a goal to write a book in 30 days. Is it realistic in terms of your schedule? Do you have kids? What about your other commitments? Again, unrealistic goals will set you up for failure.

- **Time-Bound:** All goals must have a start and an end date, but also a timeline in between. Let's say you want to write a book in six months. If the book is 18 chapters long, you will need to write three chapters per month, and just under a chapter per week. The easiest way to break this down is through word count, making sure you're writing a certain number of words per day until you've reached your goal.

Now it's time to get started on your goals and stay on track. Here are some tips I found really helpful:

Set Small Daily Goals: Overwhelm is one of the many reasons that people procrastinate. I got really excited when I started writing to-do lists—however, although it was all well and good getting the things I needed to do down on paper, I struggled to get them done. This was because I was overwhelming myself. I would write down 15-20 things to do, and then get disappointed at the end of the day when I couldn't complete them. It was my mentor who told me to cut them down to a maximum of five. I've read that ten is also a good number, but that was too much for me—it depends on how much you can handle. I found that, with five entries on my to-do list, I got them done on most days, and slowly but surely, I started to accomplish my goals.

Weekly and Monthly Goals: I was 100 pounds overweight; my weight-loss goal was to lose two pounds per week and eight pounds per month. I stuck to this and lost the 100 pounds by the end of the year! When I looked back, it didn't seem as if I'd done that much work.

Stay Focused: When you know where you want to go, and you've formulated a plan on how to get there, the task is to stay focused. It's easy to write down your goals and a plan to accomplish them—but staying focused is the difficult part. The minute you decide to get serious about your life, distractions will come from every direction. If you're not in a relationship, an ex-partner will come knocking. All at once, your friends and family members will have all these events they want you to attend. And according to Murphy's law, everything that *can* go wrong *will* go wrong. But tunnel vision is the key. Decline the invites, and work around the things that go wrong. When I started experiencing this, my biggest mistake was to try and resolve the issues before getting on with my to-do list. Big mistake! I ended up worn-out and frustrated and then unable to concentrate on my to-do list. Work on your priorities first, and everything else can wait. In other words, don't allow your problems to control you—learn how to control *them*.

Start Each Day with a Goal: As mentioned, one of my main goals was weight loss. I was too embarrassed to go to the gym, and so I would go for a 30-minute jog every morning. Exercise was difficult for me, so once I'd completed that task, I was more than motivated to move on to the rest.

Use Parkinson's Law: What happens when you think you've got all the time in the world to get stuff done? You wait until the very last minute to do it, and then you rush to complete the project. You can avoid this by using Parkinson's law; it states that the less time you've got to work on a project, the more likely you are to get it done. Use Parkinson's law by putting a timeframe on everything, and your brain will work to get the task completed within that timeframe.

Improve Your Time-Management Skills: We all have 24 hours in a day. One of the many reasons some people are successful and others are not is that high achievers use their time well. If you are going to break out of your bad habits and start getting stuff done, effective time management is an important piece of the puzzle. Here are some tips on how to improve your time-management skills:

Start Early: I am at my most productive first thing in the morning, which is why I start my day early. But I'm not the only one. As you've read, the majority of successful people start their days early. While the rest of the world is asleep, they're crushing their goals. When you wake up early, you are more calm, clearheaded, and creative. As the day goes on, your levels of motivation, focus, and productivity decrease because your energy levels are not as high. If you find it difficult to wake up early, start by getting out of bed half an hour earlier than normal. You might not think half an hour will make any difference, but it *will* because all time is valuable. You could go for a 30-minute run, write a page of your book, or work on your side hustle.

Take a Break: The body is not designed to work itself into the ground; taking regular breaks throughout the day will provide you with a steady flow of energy. When the body feels stressed, it affects your productivity. It's easy to forget to take breaks when you're the type who likes to plough through work. Avoid this by setting alarms to take 5- to 10-minute breaks every hour. During your break time, get up from your desk, walk around, or do some light stretches. But avoid checking your phone, checking social media, or surfing the Internet—it will distract you, and you'll find it difficult to get back into focus mode when you start work.

Learn to Say No: As far as I'm concerned, "No" is the most powerful word in the world, but too many people are afraid to use it in case they cause offense. I'd been a "Yes, yes" person my entire life; I didn't like conflict, and I was a people pleaser, so I'd say yes to everything. Agreeing to turn up at every social event and to help every old lady do their shopping is cute, but it's not going to get you very far in life. If time is your most valuable asset, you need to spend it wisely. You've got to get stuff done, and the only way you're going to do it is by making sure you've got enough time. This means you've got to start saying no. But be warned—people aren't going to like it, especially the ones who are used to you asking, "How high?" anytime they tell you to jump. Oh, well, whoever doesn't like it will have to deal with it in their own way. The bottom line is you'll never be able to take care of other people if you can't take care of yourself.

Avoid Multitasking: Many people take pride in their ability to multitask; they have the phone on loudspeaker while they're jumping between typing and reading a book! It's really admirable, but studies have found that it puts a dampener on your productivity. If you want to improve your time-management skills, focus on one task at a time, and you'll find that you get a lot more done throughout the day.

Stress Management: Life is stressful and there's no way for us to escape it; things happen, and we've got to deal with it in the best way we know how. The problem is that the majority of people don't know how to deal with stress, and they resort to unhealthy coping mechanisms that limit productivity and end up swallowing their time. Here are some tips for effective stress management:

- **Deep Breathing:** Pay attention to the way you breathe when you're stressed and when you're relaxed—there's a clear difference. When you're stressed, your breathing is fast and shallow; when you're relaxed, it's slow and deep. One of the most effective ways to lower stress levels is through deep breathing. When you take deep breaths, it communicates to the brain that you need to relax and calm down. This message is then sent to the body, which causes you to relax. Here is a quick deep-breathing exercise to help eliminate stress—it's called 4-7-8 breathing:

  - Take a slow, deep breath in from your stomach and count to four.

143

- When you get to four, hold your breath for seven seconds.
- Exhale all the way and count to eight.
- Repeat until you feel calm.

- **Exercise:** There are several benefits associated with exercise, including improved sleep. It also stimulates the release of the feel-good hormones endorphins, and when you feel good, stress is not going to affect you as much. Exercise also protects the body against stress because these feel-good hormones override the stress hormone cortisol.

- **Have a Conversation:** Talking therapy involves speaking with a professional counsellor to help you deal with your negative feelings. However, unless you feel that you need to speak to a professional, you can also talk to someone you trust such as a friend, relative or co-worker. The aim of talking therapy is to release negative emotions so you are not bottling them up.

Delegate Tasks: Sometimes, you've just got too much to do and not enough time in which to do it. However, by delegating tasks, you will have more time to focus on what's important. You don't need to be a manager of a multinational corporation to delegate tasks—anyone can do it. If you're a parent, delegate tasks to your children; if you're self-employed, hire a freelancer. Either way, farm out menial tasks, or the tasks you know you'll struggle with, to other people.

HOW TO STICK TO YOUR HABITS

Okay, so you've started developing good habits, and slowly but surely your old habits are falling away. But you want to make sure it stays this way. It took me about 18 months before I became truly consistent. I'm sorry to tell you that the 21-day rule doesn't work for everyone. This is especially true if you've spent the majority of your life indulging in bad habits. But what I can also tell you is that once you cross that 21-day threshold, your good habits become a lot easier to maintain. The problem is getting to that point. I would literally get to day 18 and mess up, which meant I had to go back to day one. And this just kept on happening—I couldn't make it work. I was very determined though, and on the 18th month, I hit 21 days! Whoop, whoop! So, here are some tips on how to stick to your good habits:

Choose Habits That Suit You: What do I mean by this? Well, I've always hated going to the gym, and when I was trying to lose weight, I started going to the gym—but I dreaded it. I was overweight, I had man boobs, and I just didn't feel comfortable. I would wake up every morning with anxiety, and I used that as my excuse to stop going. But when I changed my exercise regime to running, I found my mojo. I wasn't in a small, enclosed space, so I didn't feel as if people were staring at me while I struggled to keep my breath on the treadmill. I just put my earphones on and ran. I also used a running app, starting off with 5K, then moving up to 10K. Now, I run 5K every morning. Basically, if you don't like broccoli, don't force yourself to eat it—there are plenty of green vegetables out there, so find one you like. If you're not an avid reader but you want to get into the habit of reading more books, listen to audio books instead. You should also factor in your strengths, lifestyle, schedule, how complex your new habit is, your stress levels, and the time you've got available to pursue this new habit.

The Five Second Rule: In her book *The Five Second Rule*, Mel Robbins states that, as soon as you feel in your gut that you should start working on your habit or goal, you've got to get moving within five seconds—or your brain will convince you not to do it. When hesitation creeps in, count backwards from five to one, and then move. The human brain has a five-second window in which to take action; anything longer than that, and your brain will become the enemy of progress. Counting backwards acts as a distraction to the voices in your head trying to convince you of all the reasons why you should stay in bed instead of going to the gym, have a chocolate bar instead of an apple, or scroll through social media instead of writing your book. The five second rule is backed by science, and when you use it, it will radically transform your life in the same way it did mine.

The Science Behind the Five Second Rule: Metacognition is when the brain is tricked into helping you become more successful, and the five second rule falls into this category. It gives you the ability to control your brain, instead of your brain controlling you. Research suggests that approximately 40 percent of our day is spent on autopilot, which means you're living according to your preprogrammed habits. And unless you were raised in a family where success was the norm, or a military home, it's pretty likely you don't have good habits. When we are living according to our bad preprogrammed habits such as spending all our free time watching TV, eating junk food, or scrolling through social media, we are prevented from operating at our full potential. These habits keep you stuck, and you never improve.

The majority of us feel as if our lives are out of our control; when you feel like this, you limit the function of the prefrontal cortex. The prefrontal cortex is an important part of the brain responsible for working towards your goals, planning, and making decisions. To get anywhere in life, you've got to regain control of your prefrontal cortex, and you can do this by using the five second rule.

By counting down from five to one, you're being intentional about the action you're taking. It gets you out of autopilot, and the action you take gives you control over your prefrontal cortex. When you feel as if you're in the driver's seat of your life, things will start to change. As the five second rule becomes a habit, you will develop an internal locus of control—which means you believe you are totally in control of your life, your future success and outcomes. Studies indicate that those with an internal locus of control live more fulfilling lives, are more successful, and less likely to suffer from depression and anxiety.

As you continue using the five second rule, it will become easier to maintain a sense of control over your life. This is due to the principle of momentum: the amount of energy required to start something is greater than the amount of energy needed to keep it going. Life is no different; the hardest thing to do in the morning is to get out of bed and start your day—which is why most people stay under the covers until the last minute and then somehow find the energy to start rushing. However, when you use the five second rule as soon as your alarm goes off, you can beat that initial feeling of laziness. When you keep using the rule, you've moved into momentum, and this keeps pushing you forward. Think about it like a ball rolling down a hill; it will keep going until something stops it. Once you gain momentum, the only person capable of stopping you is you.

The progress principle also keeps you moving forwards; according to research conducted by Harvard Business School, the key to happiness and productivity is making progress, even if it's in small increments. Every time you use the five second rule, you're making progress, and this gives you a sense of satisfaction that drives you to keep using the rule. The five second rule creates a positive feedback loop, whereas sticking to unhealthy habits keeps you in a negative feedback loop. For example, if you have a bad habit of spending hours scrolling through social media instead of working on your goals, you feel guilty for not doing what you know you need to do. This makes you feel bad, and so you soothe yourself by scrolling through more social media. You've now activated a downward spiral of decline, and the deeper you fall into it, the harder it is to pull yourself out.

It's important to understand that you are always going to have the desire to engage in bad habits or to do the bare minimum. Having the desire to do these things isn't the problem—it only becomes a problem when you give in to these desires. This is where the five second rule becomes your superpower. When you feel the urge to do what you know you're not supposed to do, apply the rule and engage in positive behavior instead. Experts refer to this as the "Golden Rule of Habits." It's important to understand that bad habits don't disappear; you've got to replace them—and the five second rule helps you do this. The more you use the five second rule, the more you will develop what researchers call "a bias towards action." It means you have a preference towards taking action, and eventually, instead of procrastination and hesitation, the way your brain will protect you is by convincing you to take action.

Another principle that plays a role in the five second rule is that of behavioral flexibility. This is connected to locus of control and bias towards action. Studies have found that the brain is constantly developing and learning throughout life. As you keep using the five second rule and replacing bad habits with good ones, the brain develops new neural pathways, which leads to permanent behavioral change. Aristotle said it best: "Do good, be good." In other words, you can't be good if you are not going to do good; everything you want in life is on the other side of the action you take. It's not about *thinking about* what you want to do—it's about doing what you want to do. As you continue taking action and striving towards your goals, you develop "authentic pride," which means you have pride and confidence in who you are because of your personal achievements. A study conducted by the University of Columbia found that authentic pride is one of the most powerful motivators to help us reach our goals. The more pride you feel in yourself, the more motivated you feel to keep striving to achieve your goals.

There are five elements to the five second rule. Let's talk about them.

1. **Instinct:** As soon as you get that feeling in your gut that you need to work on your new habit or goal, do it. Most of us have experienced that moment when we realize we should have listened to our instincts. Like the time you had a gut feeling not to get into a relationship with that guy or girl, but you went ahead anyway, and it ended in disaster. Well, it's equally as important to act on your gut feeling when it's telling you to work on your new habit or goal. Basically, your instincts are saying, "If you don't move now, you're going to end up somewhere you don't want to be later."

2. **Act:** Pick up that apple immediately and start munching on it before your fingers start hovering over the dial button for Domino's Pizza! Our instincts are real, and studies reveal that our gut is like a mini brain—it really is trying to communicate with you. So, don't ignore it! That gut feeling is connected to your goals. Unfortunately, for most of us, it's easy to write down the things we want—but taking action to achieve them is another story. Action is one of the main ingredients when it comes to success; without putting the work in, you will never achieve your goals.

3. **Push:** There has never been a day when I've felt like waking up at 5:00 a.m. to go for a jog. Nor do I feel like writing this book. And on most days, I'd rather have a pizza than a salad! But how I feel is irrelevant because discipline is the ability to get things done whether you feel like it or not. Therefore, you've got to push yourself to do the things you don't want to do. The brain likes comfort, and it works to keep you comfortable. It's your responsibility to fight against that. You know what you need to do to change your life, and you're the only person who can do it. The five second rule sounds simple, but it's not at all. Pushing yourself into action is perhaps the most difficult thing you'll ever do.

4. **Move:** This doesn't mean you've got to start doing star jumps as soon as your instincts start talking. But it does mean you've got to start moving in the direction of your goal or new habit. *Moving* will mean whatever it means to you—it could mean putting your gym kit on, saying

what you need to say at a meeting, drinking a glass of water, or making those sales calls.

5. **Your Brain:** The brain is a wonderfully complex machine that does many great things; however, because it's been designed to protect you, it can also hinder you from achieving your goals if you don't understand how it works. The brain has three jobs: to keep your body in working order, to protect you from danger, and to store your life's memories. When you hesitate or spend a moment thinking about something, you are telling your brain that something's not quite right, and it will go into protection mode. It does this by keeping you from doing anything that feels uncertain, hard, or scary. Even though you might have some fear surrounding pursuing your dreams, you know that trying isn't going to cause you any harm—but your brain doesn't know this, which is why it tries to sabotage you.

Make a Schedule and Stick to it: Trust me—you *will* fail if you don't incorporate your habit into your schedule and stick to it. I meal-prep on Sundays because when I first started to improve my eating habits, I continuously failed miserably because I didn't have a plan. I really did want to come home and cook, but it never happened—I was too tired, so I'd buy takeaway. This went on for months until I started meal-prepping. But even then, there were some Sundays when it didn't happen, and I would be back to square one. So, I started setting my alarm clock for 12:00 p.m. on Sundays, and I've stuck to that religiously. You can set any time for yourself—just make sure it fits into your routine. Depending on what you're doing, most people find it easier to perform their new habit first thing in the morning, or just before they go to bed. Alternatively, you might find it easier to schedule time during the day.

Get Support: Success becomes easier when you've got a support network. As you know, I have an accountability partner, but if that's not possible for you, a good support network amongst your friends and family can be a great help. You might find that someone wants to join you, which is even better. It's always nice to have a healthy-eating partner or a workout partner. A support network will keep you going on the days you don't feel like it.

Make Sure You're Staying on Track: I kept a list of my daily routine and a 21-day checklist pinned to a noticeboard in my bedroom. I would look at the list first thing in the morning and before I went to bed at night. When I had completed everything on my routine, I would tick off each day. When I failed, I wrote out another 21-day checklist and started again. This way, I always knew how many days I had left, and it pushed me to keep going even though I failed several times. I got there in the end.

By now you should know what your bad habits are, and what you need to do to change them. However, you might be at a bit of a loss about some of the good habits you need to adopt. So, in the final chapter, I'll provide you with some options.

CHAPTER 11:

HEALTHY HABITS TO ADOPT

I f you are anything like me, there are probably a lot of things you are doing right now that you don't know are bad for you. For example, I've always been a sloucher, and it wasn't until my mentor pulled me up on it that I made a conscious decision to change the habit. To give you a helping hand, I'm going to end the book with a list of healthy habits you can adopt. Have a read through the list and see what you could apply that would benefit you.

Be More Positive: You are what you think, so if you have a habit of seeing the worst in everything, being too critical, or thinking negative thoughts all the time, you're probably not a very happy person. Now, don't take that the wrong way, but it's the reality of the situation. Negative thinking leads to a downward spiral of decline—trust me; I've seen good friends break up because one friend thought the other wasn't supporting them because they were not liking their Instagram posts! Sounds ridiculous but it happens. Let me break it down. You post some good news, and your best friend doesn't like the post. What is your first thought? That maybe they didn't see it? They saw it but forgot to like it? Or they ignored the post because they were hating and being mean and spiteful? In the scenario above, you immediately jumped to the conclusion that the post wasn't liked because the other friend was hating and being mean and spiteful. You kept thinking about it, got worked up and decided to confront your friend. The friend says she didn't see it, but you are convinced she did. Well, that's a really stupid assumption because unless you were there to actually see your friend scroll past it, and inside your friend's head to see that she was hating, there is no way you can possibly come to that conclusion. Therefore, since you don't have all the facts, the best way to deal with it is to assume your friend didn't see the post, or they saw it and forgot to like it. No big deal—it's only a like, right?

Smile More Often: Smiling improves your overall mental well-being. There are some days when you just don't feel like smiling. But according to research, feel-good hormones are released when you smile, and even if you fake it, the brain can't tell the difference, so the feel-good hormones are released anyway. Make a habit of smiling, and you'll notice how much better you feel, even on the bad days.

Snuggle with Your Partner: Relationships take work. When the initial chemistry wears off, you've got to put the effort in to keep your union strong. One way you can do this is through snuggling. Physical touch influences how you feel about your partner because hugging triggers the release of the love and bonding hormone oxytocin. In other words, you can quickly spice up your love life by making a habit of hugging your partner.

Step Out of Your Comfort Zone: Growth doesn't happen in comfortable surroundings. If you want to be successful, you've got to get comfortable with being uncomfortable. Write a list of all the things you don't enjoy—for example, I can't stand swimming, but now I go swimming once a week. Start doing things you don't enjoy, and it will help you push boundaries and expand in other areas of your life.

Practice Mindfulness: Most of us don't live in the present moment; we either live in the past or in the future. A lot of us waste time regretting something we did last week, or feeling anxious about something that's happening in a month's time. We can be having a face-to-face conversation with someone but thinking about what we're going to eat for dinner. Mindfulness involves being fully present by participating in the moment without thinking about anything else.

Improve Your Body Language: Experts suggest that we speak louder with our body language than we do with our words. A lot of our body language is unconscious, and we may unintentionally give off the wrong messages because of it. Body language is either positive or negative; therefore, make a conscious decision to study yours, and put more positive body language into practice.

Do Things Alone: Have you ever been to the cinema alone? How about out to a restaurant? Many people don't feel comfortable doing things alone because they either don't like being by themselves, or they're worried about what other people are going to think about them. But the ability to enjoy your own company is a very powerful quality to have. It's an indication that you'll never settle for less when it comes to being in a relationship.

Detox Often: And I don't mean a physical detox—I mean a mental one. Every once in a while, detox from things such as social media, watching YouTube videos, or watching TV. The digital world is great, but it becomes a problem when you feel as if you can't live without it. Being online all the time can also take away from your ability to live in the present moment. And even worse, there is a growing body of evidence that says it can have a negative effect on your mental health.

Do a Relationship Cleanse: First of all, it's important to understand that some people come into your life like the seasons; they are temporary, not permanent. They served a specific purpose at a certain time, and now it's time to let them go. Also, it's easy to learn to deal with toxic friends and family members—I've been there, done that, and worn the T-shirt. But if you allow them to keep taking up space in your life, they will hinder you from getting where you need to go. Every so often, do a relationship cleanse; either cut these people off completely, or keep them at arm's length.

Eat Less: I was amazed to find that when you're healthy, your stomach is the size of a fist. When you're unhealthy, your stomach is the size of a football! That's a massive (pun not intended) difference. Basically, overeating causes the stomach to expand, and when this is done consistently, the stomach stretches and stays that way. As a result, you've got to eat more than you usually would to feel satisfied. You can avoid this by not eating so much. Most people eat until they're stuffed and can't breathe. Take some advice from the Japanese culture: eat until you're only 80 percent full. If your stomach is already stretched, like mine, this will get it back to its original size. Eating less will also prevent your stomach from expanding, and help you maintain a healthy weight.

Freeze Your Fruits: You can freeze fruits such as blueberries, strawberries, bananas, pineapple, and mango and use them for smoothies. This way, you can buy them in bulk, and they won't go off.

Walk More: Unless you've got a medical condition that prevents you from walking, you can drastically increase your activity levels by walking more. Instead of using the elevator, use the stairs; if you take the bus to work, walk to the next bus stop instead of going to the one outside your house. After you've finished your lunch, go for a quick walk.

Weigh Yourself Once a Week: Sometimes, weight gain isn't obvious; it creeps up on you until you go to wear your favorite pair of jeans, and you can't get the zipper up. You can avoid this by stepping on the scales once a week. Now, I'm not encouraging you to obsess over your weight, but excess weight can cause several health problems, and that's the last thing you need.

Get a Dog: When someone is dependent on you, it triggers a drive to do more. Obviously, this good habit is only for those of you who love dogs, but if you're struggling to get into a routine or to exercise more, a dog will help you do so. Dogs need routine to thrive; you've got to feed them, take them on walks, bathe and groom them. If you find exercising difficult, taking your dog for a walk every day can also become your exercising time. Feeding your dog will serve as a reminder to eat something healthy.

Well, that's about all for now. I hope you've gained some inspiration from this chapter, and that you're ready to transform your life and start implementing some of the habits mentioned above.

CONCLUSION

I really wish I could tell you how easy this is going to be. That you can start your journey today, and tomorrow you'll have a mind of steel and the self-discipline of the late Kobe Bryant. But unfortunately, that would be a gigantic lie, and I can't do that to you. The truth is that breaking your bad habits and adopting good ones is going to be the most difficult thing you'll ever do because, as I've mentioned throughout this book, they've become a part of you, and it's all you know. Statistics say that the majority of people give up within a month. I'd like to have a bit more faith in you than that.

I was almost a statistic; I kept giving up—it was too hard! I liked eating junk food, spending money recklessly, and acting on impulse. And I most certainly could have lived the rest of my life this way. But I wasn't happy, and I knew that the only way to experience true joy was to live my dreams. I couldn't do that if I didn't have any discipline. I had to make a choice, and I had to do so quickly. Les Brown was one of the people who kept motivating me to keep going. In one of his speeches, he presented a scenario of being on your deathbed, and instead of having your loved ones surrounding you, you are visited by your dreams. They are angry with you because you didn't give them the opportunity to live, and now they've got to go to the grave with you. That's what will happen if you don't change your habits. Everything you've ever wanted will remain a dream. One day, you'll wake up and realize you've completely wasted your life, and by then, it might be too late.

This book has all the information you're ever going to need to transform your life. There is no easy way around it. I was one of those people who kept reading books like this hoping to find an easier option. When I found out about visualization, I was over the moon. "Great!" I thought to myself. "I can just think my way to success." When that didn't work, I moved on to speaking things into existence. When that didn't work, I moved on to the 555 Method! My point is that there are no shortcuts—I've tried everything, and nothing worked until I changed my habits and got serious about making things happen by becoming action oriented. If you want to see results, you've got to put the work in. Wishing upon a star isn't going to cut it!

The best way to start changing your habits is to start small. Don't make plans to transform your life overnight—your brain won't be able to handle it, and you'll give up very quickly. But I promise you that if you can be consistent for three months—and I mean maintain a routine every day for ninety days—you'll succeed in whatever you're trying to accomplish. Remember, discipline is a muscle, and if you put some pressure on it, it will grow. It's going to feel very uncomfortable in the beginning because the job of your subconscious mind is to ensure that you're comfortable. When you start acting contrary to your mental programming, your mind will fight you to stick to what it knows. Everything in you is going to want to hit the snooze button, eat another burger, and spend money you don't have, but the more you resist, the easier it will become. I failed several times before I nailed it. I kept writing out "21 days" in big red letters; I'd get through the first three days, and flunk on the fourth. So, I had to go back to day one. I needed to convince myself that each day of failure was taking me back to square one. As I mentioned earlier, it took me 18 months to keep a routine for 21 days! But once I hit those 21 days, getting to 90 days was a breeze. The choice is yours: You can either live with the pain of regret, or you can endure the pain of perseverance.

I wish you every success as you embark on this new journey to replace your bad habits with good ones and live the fulfilling and fantastic life you were destined for.

THANKS FOR READING!

I really hope you enjoyed this book and, most of all, got more from it than you had to give.

It would mean a lot to me if you left an Amazon review—I will reply to all questions asked!

Simply find this book on Amazon, scroll to the reviews section, and click "Write a customer review".

Or Scan the QR Code on Your Phone:

Be sure to check out my email list, where I am constantly adding tons of value. The best way to currently get on the list is by visiting www.pristinepublish.com/morningbonus and entering your email address.

Here, I'll provide actionable information that aims to increase your enjoyment of life. I'll update you on my latest books, and I'll even send free e-books that I think you'll find useful.

Kindest regards,

Daniel Walter

ALSO BY

Daniel Walter

Discover how to easily master focus and productivity to uplevel your life in ways you never expected.

Visit: www.pristinepublish.com/daniel

Or Scan the QR Code on Your Phone:

REFERENCES

Anon, (2020). *Research Paper: Neuroscience Behind Creating A Habit – Simplified.*

Centers for Disease Control and Prevention (2019). *CDC - sleep home page - sleep and sleep disorders.*

Clear, J. (2019). *Atomic Habits: An Easy & Proven Way to Build Good Habits and Break Bad Ones* (01 ed.). Penguin Random House USA.

Covey, S. R. (2020). *The 7 Habits of Highly Effective People: 30th Anniversary Edition* (4th ed.). Simon & Schuster.

Cross, R., Wright, C., & Hensley, G. (2019). *Habits of a Happy Brain: The Only Two Books You Will Ever Need to Discover What Neuroscience Says About Habit Formation, to Build Strong Habits and to Achieve the Success You Deserve.* Richard Cross.

DePaul, K. (2021). *What Does It Really Take to Build a New Habit?* Harvard Business Review.

Edblad, P. (2016). *The Habit Blueprint: 15 Simple Steps to Transform Your Life (The Good Life Blueprint Series).*

Elrod, H. (2018). *The Miracle Morning: The 6 Habits That Will Transform Your Life Before 8AM.* Teach Yourself.

Fiore, N. (2007). *The Now Habit: A Strategic Program for Overcoming Procrastination and Enjoying Guilt-Free Play* (Revised ed.). TarcherPerigee.

Fontana, L., Partridge, L. and Longo, V.D. (2010). Extending Healthy Life Span--From Yeast to Humans. *Science,* 328(5976), pp.321–326.

Fritz, R. (2011). *The Path of Least Resistance for Managers* (Second ed.). Newfane Press.

Frontiersin.org. (2019). *Article | Frontiers.*

Gardner, B., Lally, P. and Wardle, J. (2012). Making health habitual: the psychology of 'habit-formation' and general practice. *British Journal of General Practice,* 62(605), pp.664–666.

Graziosi, D. (2019). *Millionaire Success Habits: The Gateway to Wealth & Prosperity* (Illustrated ed.). Hay House Inc.

Groopman, J. (2019). *Can Brain Science Help Us Break Bad Habits?* The New Yorker.

Houston, E. (2016). Changing Habits for the Long Haul. *APS Observer.*

Judah, G., Gardner, B., Kenward, M.G., DeStavola, B. and Aunger, R. (2018). Exploratory study of the impact of perceived reward on habit formation. *BMC Psychology.*

Marien, H., Custers, R. and Aarts, H. (2019). Studying Human Habits in Societal Context: Examining Support for a

Basic Stimulus–Response Mechanism. *Current Directions in Psychological Science.*

McGonigal, K. (2013). *The Willpower Instinct: How Self-Control Works, Why It Matters, and What You Can Do to Get More of It* (Illustrated ed.). Avery.

Neal, D. T., Wood, W., Labrecque, J. S. and Lally, P. (2012). How do habits guide behavior? Perceived and actual triggers of habits in daily life. *Journal of Experimental Social Psychology*, 48(2), pp.492–498.

Parker, S. (2021). The science of habits. *Knowable Magazine | Annual Reviews.*

PhD, F. B. J. (2021). *Tiny Habits: The Small Changes That Change Everything* (1st ed.). Mariner Books.

Rubin, G., Rubin, B. T. B. B. G., 978–0385348638, Rubin, F. T. B. G., & 978–1473663701. (2021). *Gretchen Rubin 2 Books Collection Set (Better Than Before, The Four Tendencies).* Two Roads.

Schwartz, J. M., & Md, G. R. (2012). *You Are Not Your Brain: The 4-Step Solution for Changing Bad Habits, Ending Unhealthy Thinking, and Taking Control of Your Life* (Reprint ed.). Avery.

ScienceDaily. (n.d.). *How we form habits, change existing ones.*

Sinek, S., Mead, D., & Docker, P. (2017). *Find Your Why: A Practical Guide for Discovering Purpose for You and Your Team* (Illustrated ed.). Portfolio.

Made in the USA
Las Vegas, NV
13 December 2024

14115564R00095